LISMORE CASTLE

LISMORE CASTLE

FOOD AND FLOWERS FROM A HISTORIC IRISH GARDEN

LAURA BURLINGTON

Texts by William Burlington,
Eliza Wood, Colm O'Driscoll,
Kelly Mason, and Lee Behegan
Photography by Anna Batchelor
Recipes by Teena Mahon

RIZZOLI
NEW YORK

New York · Paris · London · Milan

Above: William and Laura Burlington with their family dogs, Pins and Needles; pages 16–17: View of Lismore Castle from the bridge designed by eighteenth-century Irish architect Thomas Ivory and commissioned by the fifth Duke of Devonshire.

Contents

Recipes

Introduction
Laura Burlington

For many years, people have asked for a book about Lismore Castle. The gardens of the castle were opened by my husband William's grandparents in the 1960s, and each year many visitors from around the world make the journey to see them. William opened the gallery known as Lismore Castle Arts in a derelict wing in 2005, and garden visitors have been joined by those on contemporary art pilgrimages. Once a year we open the gallery and gardens for the season, and the castle is full of artists, friends and supporters. This book explains our approach to looking after and celebrating our guests. It is my experience that the interiors of Lismore—a combination of gothic patterns and clutter, some of it modern, some of it old, some of it good and some of it won at the local fair—immediately make people feel comfortable. It is all gathered and presented with equal importance, and because no one family has lived full-time in the main part of the castle since Adele Astaire's tenure, no one has ever cleared it up. In fact, you are still able to find Adele's records on the sideboards and her novels on the bookshelves. The castle itself is not open to the public except when rented as a whole, and I hope this book will open the doors and give readers a glimpse of Lismore's eclectic style.

The castle has such a particular atmosphere, and one of my worries as one of the present incumbents is how not to spoil this. It was sensitively refurbished at the beginning of the century by my parents-in-law, who added significantly to the collection of Pugin furniture and Watts wallpaper that feels so very at home here. I find it quite difficult to change anything in the castle. The doors, for example, have a particularly strange, brown stippling effect the likes of which I've never seen anywhere else, a bit as if they have been painted with treacle toffee. A moment arose when they needed some attention, and after much head-scratching about all the possibilities of how to paint them and the different colours that could work, when it came down to it, I just settled on new brown toffee stippling.

The gardens are a different matter altogether. Their beauty is that they are constantly dynamic—living, dying and aggressively growing, with even the most reticent shrub becoming too big in the soft Irish climate. A surprising moment of freedom arrived with box blight, when we were forced to remove all the formal box hedging in the garden. As a consequence, a much looser perennial style has become Lismore's latest look.

The kitchen garden supplies most of the fruits and vegetables that we eat in the house, and no book about Lismore could really exist without talking about that food and its short journey to the kitchen. Teena, the castle's cook, has developed a style that moves through the seasons, working with what has grown and is available, and including some of the favourites that one would hope to find in an Irish house. Porridge, soda bread and stews are staples (and you will find recipes for them enclosed), but Teena also makes the freshest salads and jams and chutneys to deal with the inevitable glut of homegrown vegetables. Despite my best efforts, tea remains a substantial meal in itself. At times I have tried to reduce it, but this has always been met with considerable resistance.

The flowers in the house celebrate the changing of the seasons. Everything grows so quickly in Ireland that while in other places you might think twice about hacking off the branch of a magnolia to place it in a vase, it is not something that would ever bother you in this warm, wet climate. For many centuries Lismore has been the backdrop for celebrations, comings together and conversations—often late into the evening—so we thought that we should also include a few cocktails in this book.

Lismore is a place made extraordinary by those who work there, by those who care for the house and its gardens and by the visitors who pass through its doors.

Above the fireplace in the banqueting hall is written *céad míle fáilte*, Gaelic for 'one hundred thousand welcomes', and short of making the journey, we hope this book extends the same welcome through the following pages.

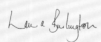

Following pages: The Drawing Room with eighteenth-century Teniers tapestries portraying scenes from *Don Quixote*.

A Short History of Lismore Castle
William Burlington

'Nor in any country that I have visited have I seen a view more noble – it is too rich and peaceful to be what is called romantic, but lofty, large and generous, if the term may be used; the river and banks as fine as the Rhine'.
- William Makepeace Thackeray on Lismore,
The Irish Sketchbook of 1842.

Lismore Castle is over eight hundred years old. During that time, it has been bought and sold, attacked and defended, occupied and relinquished, destroyed and rebuilt.

It has played host to artists, authors, actors, presidents, princes and kings. And it has been home to bishops and dukes, gardeners and gatekeepers, and one Hollywood star. In short, it is a place full of stories—some happy, some sad.

I first came to Lismore for two days in 1979 when I was aged ten, and it was like a dream—a dream filled with turrets and cannonballs, mist and moss, and green everywhere. There was a place where one could feel an actual cannonball lodged in a defensive wall—if one was brave enough to put one's hand deep into a dark hole. And I remember another cannonball being used as a doorstop. I fell in love, and that love has endured.

Lios Mór means 'great fort' in Irish. Lismore's location, looking down over the River Blackwater, is significant because the original castle was built in 1185 to defend a crossing place. It was built on the site of Lismore Abbey— a religious settlement and a seat of learning founded by Saint Mochuda, or Carthage, in the seventh century—and was used for some years as a bishop's residence.

For much of the medieval period Lismore was in the hands of the earls of Desmond, and for a short while it was owned by Sir Walter Raleigh, who

Opposite: The gatehouse, one of the oldest parts of Lismore Castle, featuring the crests of the Boyle and Fenton families.

sold the estate to Richard Boyle in 1602. Boyle, who became first Earl of Cork in 1620, was a significant and notorious figure in Irish history. He made Lismore Castle his principal residence and undertook major rebuilding work, transforming it into one of the largest houses in Ireland. His coat of arms and motto, 'God's providence is my inheritance', can still be seen carved into the stone of the gatehouse entrance that he built.

The earl had fifteen children in all, eleven of whom survived to adulthood. They included Robert Boyle, who became a leading intellectual figure of the seventeenth century and one of the founders of modern chemistry, born at the castle on 25 January 1627, and his sister and scientific collaborator Katherine Boyle, later Lady Ranelagh.

It is possible that the yew avenue in the lower garden dates from this time. Edmund Spenser is said to have written part of his allegorical poem 'The Faerie Queene' in the grounds of the castle; however, this, like certain other aspects of Lismore's history, may belong more rightfully under the heading of myth, rather than reality. When one steps past the ancient trees and walls surrounding the castle, on the same paths that might have been trodden by saints—and certainly by sinners—the imagination can all too easily take hold, and the division between myth and reality becomes an irrelevance.

The 1640s saw turbulent times in Ireland, and the castle was besieged twice, the second time successfully, leaving it 'ruinated' according to the civil survey of 1654–56. Nevertheless, the castle and associated estates were retained by the Earl of Cork's successors, and in 1753 the inheritance passed to the earl's descendant Charlotte Boyle and her husband, William Cavendish, the future fourth Duke of Devonshire. It has remained with the Devonshire family ever since.

In 1811 at the age of twenty-one, William Cavendish, the sixth Duke of Devonshire, inherited eight significant estates in England and Ireland, including Lismore. Not long after, he commissioned William Atkinson to remodel some of the rooms in the castle's north wing, and reputedly it was around this time that workmen discovered a twelfth-century bishop's crozier and a fifteenth-century Gaelic manuscript, known as the Book of Lismore (or more accurately the book of Mac Cárthaigh Riabhach), behind a walled-up doorway. These remarkable artefacts are now to be found in the more accessible locations of, respectively, the National Museum of Ireland in Dublin and University College Cork.

By 1844 almost half of the duke's income was being used to pay interest on inherited mortgages and loans, including some of his late mother's gambling debts. On top of this, the duke had extravagant tastes of his own. In July of that year, a proposal was made to the duke. The proposal included selling his Irish castle and estate, which had not been lived in by the family for over one hundred years. However, the duke had no desire to part with the castle. Encouraged by his cousin and trustee George Cavendish, he eventually decided instead to sell two estates in Yorkshire and devote significant attention—and funds—to Lismore.

The duke was the first family member in many years to visit Lismore regularly. The 1850s saw a grand scheme of rebuilding designed and overseen by architect, engineer and gardener Sir Joseph Paxton. Apart from Atkinson's principal rooms in the north range and the Earl of Cork's gatehouse, the entire castle was altered. The interiors were devised by John Gregory Crace, often using the designs of Augustus Pugin.

Paxton and the duke's vision was far from timid. The result was the imposing neogothic castle—or as the duke described it to his sister, 'this quasi-feudal ultra-regal fortress'—that survives today. Responsibility for managing the renovations fell to the duke's land agent, Francis Edmund Currey, a pioneering amateur photographer, among other things. Currey's daughter Fanny Currey, born in Lismore, was a horticulturalist and artist and a founding member of what later became the Watercolour Society of Ireland. Her work hangs in the castle to this day.

The duke was an enthusiastic host. One of his more memorable events at Lismore was the ball that he gave for his niece the Duchess of Sutherland and her daughter Lady Constance Leveson-Gower in 1851. The celebrations included fireworks, races on the river and music provided by the phenomenon that was the Joseph Richardson and Sons Rock, Bell and Steel Band.

Following pages: A collection of images taken from Chatsworth's archives. Clockwise from left: The Riding House, 1964. Built in 1631 and 1632, it was made with stone quarried on the estate; Admiring the catch; Yew Avenue, 1964; Duchess Deborah on her horse, Royal Tan, a Grand National winner given to the Duchess by Aly Khan. The Sitting Room, circa 1960s. In the early 2000s, the swimming pool installed by Adele Astaire in the 1930s was filled in. Spencer Compton Cavendish, eighth Duke of Devonshire, fishing on the banks of the Blackwater, circa 1900.

In 1855, Paxton ('the Nuns dote on him', recorded the duke in his diary) paid his last visit to Lismore, and on the duke's death in 1858 all building work ceased.

The family continued to live in England but would visit Lismore regularly, often spending up to three months of the year there. They hosted numerous guests there over the years, including in 1904 King Edward VII and Queen Alexandra.

During the Irish Civil War in 1922, the castle was briefly taken over and occupied by Republican forces. They stayed for twenty-five days, during which kerosene was poured over floors and curtains in preparation for its burning—the fate of approximately two hundred large houses in Ireland around that time.

In the end the castle was not destroyed; however, it sustained considerable damage. Evidence of this can still be seen—yet another powerful layer of the castle's complex history.

Subsequent custodians have not undertaken programmes of work on the scale of the Earl of Cork or the sixth Duke of Devonshire, although the family have continued to visit Lismore. Between 1932 and 1944 the castle was continually occupied by Lord Charles Cavendish and his wife, Adele Astaire, dancer, actress and sister of Fred. Lord Charles was given the castle by his father, the ninth Duke of Devonshire, as the inheritance of a second son. Adele was true Hollywood A-list, and they lived a celebrity lifestyle. Fred Astaire was a regular visitor. He loved fishing, and he loved talking horses in one or another of the thirteen pubs of Lismore.

During their tenure, Charles and Adele built a swimming pool, a tennis court and a squash court—not standard fare in this part of Ireland at the time. They also brought the castle's waterworks into the twentieth century. The writer Patrick Leigh Fermor wrote to my grandmother that 'Lismore Castle was built by King John, plumbed by Adele Astaire!'

Lord Charles died young, and there were no surviving children, so Adele moved back to the United States, where she remarried. She often returned

Opposite: Fred and Adele Astaire at Lismore Castle, August 1975.

FRED & ADELE

to Lismore with her new husband, Kingman Douglass, but the castle's Hollywood moment was over, and it became once again part of the Devonshire family inheritance.

This inheritance, along with a heavy tax burden, fell to my grandfather Andrew Cavendish on the death of his father in 1950. With his wife, Deborah Mitford, Andrew used to make annual visits to Lismore and brought friends and relatives to stay. The future U.S. president John F Kennedy came in 1947, and the guestbook for the time records various artists, authors and other politicians.

Ireland was free from the Second World War food rationing that remained in place in Britian until 1958, so it was a place of comparative luxury for those who could afford it. However, there was no money for repairs. An outbreak of dry rot in one wing of the castle was dealt with by pulling the plaster off all the walls and leaving them open to the air. The novelist L. P. Hartley visited and recorded what he found in his bedroom, including that there was a 'pair of soapstone bookends with no books between them'.

In the 1990s my grandfather Andrew passed on the responsibility of overseeing Lismore to my parents. They were not burdened by debt, but the castle had been chronically underfunded for almost a century, so there was still quite a challenge ahead of them. Over time the family's UK business interests had started to generate some surplus that they were able to use to benefit Lismore. They worked with Melissa Wyndham and Jonathan Bourne to renovate the interiors and return the castle from the threadbare and drafty place it had become to a place of great luxury and style. Local restorers and specialists were used where possible, and contemporary sculpture was introduced into the garden.

One major element of Lismore Castle's history that has not been properly written about—yet—is that of the people who have tended the house and the gardens, day in day out, over the centuries, sometimes making it their life's work. It would take a more thorough history—and historian—to cover this topic effectively, but one name stands out above all, a legendary figure for anyone who has known Lismore over the past few decades: Denis Nevin, whose blood runs in the castle's veins. Clerk of works, butler, tour

32

leader, host and much more besides, Denis had a significant involvement in my parents' 1990s renovations. Denis has a rare combination of the artist's sensibilities with the craftsman's practicality and resourcefulness. And it is not only my family who have benefitted from Denis's presence at Lismore, because since the 1980s the castle has been available for private hire by guests from all over the world, and Denis has been there to welcome everybody. Some guests have regularly brought family and friends to the castle for many years—spanning five decades and four generations in the case of the Fitzpatricks—and have thus written their own chapters of Lismore's history.

As I write, the Cavendish family connection with Lismore is as strong as ever. Since 2007 my wife, Laura, and I have had the honour of being the family custodians of the castle, our home from home in Ireland. From a personal point of view, we have had some of the happiest times of our lives at Lismore, including my sister's wedding, our own wedding party and the christening of one of our children. But more than that, circumstances have enabled us to open the castle, to ensure the walls that were built to keep people out now welcome people in.

The garden has been open to visitors since the 1960s, and there is now a nonprofit art gallery, Lismore Castle Arts, in the once-derelict west wing, with a busy programme of supporting events. Every year we organise a children's literary festival and host an opera festival on the castle grounds, as well as numerous school visits, workshops and other cultural activities. And the castle is regularly used for local fundraisers and receptions, most recently the launch of the official history of Lismore GAA.

At Lismore the layers of history overlap and intertwine, they clash and they elide. There might be an abstract sculpture to one side of you, a piece of the Berlin Wall on the other, and it is not difficult to imagine the inhabitants of the past, or even the Vikings who came up the river in search of gold, in the rooms. And if you do find it hard to summon up such images, there is still a cannonball being used as a doorstop to remind you.

William Burlington

Opposite: A collection of Richard Long's works on old slates from the roof of the castle; following pages: Two sections of the Berlin Wall, acquired by William Burlington in 2015; pages 38–39: The lower garden.

Interiors

Each generation that takes up residence at Lismore leaves their mark upon the place. The layers of history are hardly better represented than in the physical layers of furniture, fabrics and decoration which are so often added to rather than replaced. The interiors as they stand now are a blend of tastes over many years, though the castle's most recent major renovation was carried out by the twelfth duke and duchess, my parents-in-law, in the early 2000s. Denis Nevin remembers when he first came to the castle in 1977 that only 40 percent of the rooms were habitable. The main house and Cork wing were to be avoided, as they were structurally unsafe, and only a handful of rooms had radiators. Heating was extended by my parents-in-law, which was a huge undertaking. Duchess Amanda recalls setting about the redecoration with furniture specialist Jonathan Bourne and interior decorator Melissa Wyndham.

The aim was to preserve the sixth duke's intentions while bringing the castle into the twenty-first century. Still, they were not starting from scratch, as the castle and its previous inhabitants left clues for its new direction all around. During one visit to the castle attics, they found some old curtains in a bag. After some digging, they discovered it was the pair of curtains portrayed in Samuel Cook's watercolour of the entrance hall in the 1850s. Though they were no longer fit for purpose as curtains, much of the fabric was salvaged and repurposed to cover the front of a cupboard that now stands a few feet away from Cook's painting depicting them.

On further exploration of the attics and basements, my parents-in-law rediscovered several items of furniture designed for Lismore by Augustus Pugin, the architect and designer who is celebrated for his Gothic Revival style, during the sixth duke's extensive works to the castle in the nineteenth century. Lismore supposedly has the largest private domestic collection of Pugin furniture in the world today. Beyond the sixth duke's original commission, thanks are also due to Duchess Evelyn, wife of the ninth duke. Despite not liking the furniture herself, she knew it would surely come back in fashion, and wisely chose to store it in the basements for future generations. This acclaim is also due to some sleuth work by my parents-in-law, who added to the pre-existing collection of Pugin furniture. One bookcase was found for sale in Australia, having been taken there among the possessions of an archbishop at some point.

Previous page: The entrance lobby; opposite: The entrance hall. A portrait of William Spencer Cavendish (1790–1858), the sixth Duke of Devonshire, at the top of the stairs, painted in 1850 and 1851 by British artist Sir Francis Grant.

It is said that one of the original spurs that encouraged the sixth duke to lend attention to the developments at Lismore was a near scathing review from his cousin Lady Caroline Lamb. In 1812, following a bout of heartbreak, the duke whisked his cousin away to what she expected to be a romantic castle able to cure aching hearts. However, upon arriving at Lismore, Lady Caroline professed that it was 'not a gothic hall, but two small dapper parlours neatly furnished in the newest Inn fashion' and complained of its being very damp. Work began immediately, and the next decade would see a string of improvements, including extensive reroofing and restoration, as the castle began its gothicised, medieval-revival renovation. Between the constant string of parties, music recitals and dances that filled much of the duke's time, he and Paxton turned their attention to the conversion of the ruined chapel into an impressive banqueting hall in 1850 and 1851. Paxton drew up the architectural plans and brought in the acclaimed decorator of the time John Gregory Crace to lead the decoration. Crace in turn introduced Pugin to the project to create gothic-style furniture.

Paxton, who was busy with several projects back home in England, sent John Brown, head mason at Chatsworth House—which remains our family's main home in England—to be his man on the ground at Lismore. Brown oversaw the successful manoeuvring of the stone for the windows and doorways. The stone had been quarried and cut to measure at Chatsworth and then transported via private ferry and canal to Lismore. The metalwork and stained glass were made by Hardman of Birmingham and the fireplace tiles by Minton.

Remarkably, the room today is much as it was when first completed; the pew-like benches that run around the perimeter of the room, a nod to the space's original function as a chapel during Robert Boyle's time, have new fabric to cover seat pads, but are otherwise untouched. They were built to serve as a respite for the duke's guests when wearied in the 'mazy circles of dance', according to one of the newspapers of the time, and nowadays are used as overflow seating when the hall is filled for the many events it hosts.

The chimneypiece (seen in the photo on page 160), perhaps the most impressive feature of the room, was displayed in the Medieval Court of the Great Exhibition in 1851 which was hosted in the Crystal Palace in London, designed by Joseph Paxton. The chimneypiece itself was designed by Pugin for another home; it was due for Horsted Place in Sussex, but the story goes it was rejected for being too elaborate—not a problem for the Devonshires—and family crests were quickly changed before it was installed in Lismore. The elaborately carved and twisted brass chandelier is also from the Great Exhibition.

The stained glass, made by Hardman of Birmingham, illustrates Saint Patrick and Saint George, the patron saints of Ireland and England respectively. The crests on the wall belong to the Boyle and Fenton families and are the same as those carved in stone above the front gate outside the castle.

This was perhaps part of the inspiration that Hugh Kennedy gathered from the castle when he came to make two chandeliers commissioned by my parents-in-law. Like Pugin, he used motifs from branches of the family, including Cavendish, Clifford and Hardwick, as well as Carter and Dunne for William's two brothers-in-law. However, Kennedy also included some jokes to test the historians of the future; among the sixteen crests one can see the gavels representing Sotheby's, where my father-in-law worked at the time, and any global football fan will recognize (and hopefully admire) the white and red gun motif of Arsenal FC. Also included are Bourne and Wyndham to remember the fond days of discovery and decorating.

The dining room is one of the hardest working rooms in the castle. It is where guests meet for breakfast, lunch and usually dinner. It has been home to several Pugin pieces since they were originally designed for Lismore, including all the dining chairs, which bear the Devonshire crest. The sideboard is one of the most impressive and elaborate surviving pieces at Lismore. It was the topic of much correspondence between Pugin and Crace; the latter believed that the design proposed by Pugin needed to be improved upon by adding drawers or cupboards, to which Pugin responded, 'The design you sent down was made for a small sideboard for a small man but a grand fellow is supposed to have other places to keep his things than the sideboard'. My parents-in-law added to the room by hanging paintings from more recent times by Stephen Conroy and Peter Frie, which rub shoulders with some seventeenth-century oils. The carpet is from a design

Following pages: The Banqueting Hall.

by Pugin that my mother-in-law found in a book. The team commissioned Avena Carpets to make an exact replica. Charlie Trigg, a metalworker from Lismore, was commissioned to make a set of log baskets with motifs reminiscent of Lismore for each of the large entertainment rooms, including the dining room.

The wallpaper, which acts as the endpapers of this book, has its own comical tale: it originally arrived in the wrong colour, and the mistake was picked up just in time as the paste was being prepped on the walls. The miscoloured batch could not be returned to Cole & Son to be redistributed elsewhere, and some is found in Careysville House, a fishing lodge perched above the River Blackwater, sixteen miles upstream from Lismore, purchased by the eleventh duke.

The white ceiling was the work of Duchess Evelyn, who made several of her own alterations to the interiors of the castle. Most notably—and perhaps controversially—she covered over the decorative painted ceiling on the basis that it was too oppressive. However, given the vast amount of pattern and detail in the room, and the lack of decent lighting in the beginning of the twentieth century, one can hardly blame her for quietening the room and wanting to bounce some natural light across the ceiling. She was also known to paint some pieces of Pugin furniture, and she cut a section out of a tapestry in the sitting room to make it fit above the alcove of the door. This might not have been done in today's climate, but it is this act that resulted in one of the most interesting elements of the house, much admired and loved by guests. She also did many of the repairs herself, and often found resourceful ways around what could be painstaking tasks, including painting a section of the sitting room tapestry onto canvas rather than restitching it.

As William mentions, in Ireland postwar life did not involve rationing like it did in England, and therefore Lismore became the obvious destination for members of the family to entertain more freely. In September 1947, then congressman John F Kennedy landed in Ireland for a three-week stay with his sister Kathleen, known as Kick to family and friends. She had married Billy Cavendish, elder son of the tenth Duke of Devonshire, in 1944 and was tragically widowed after only four months of marriage. However, she was still given the use of Lismore for holidays. As Ryan Tubridy notes in

Opposite: A writing desk in the drawing room with views out to the Blackwater River. A circa 1844 portrait of Sir Joseph Paxton by Thomas Ellerby sits above a portrait of William Spencer Cavendish as Marquess of Hartington.

his book about the future president's trip to follow his Irish roots to their humble beginnings, he spent the day with a close relative and 'left in a flow of nostalgia and sentiment'. When back at the castle, he thought about his cousin's cottage as he looked down the dining table and said to himself, 'What a contrast!'

Nick Prioleau, who worked as the estate's agent in the 1950s for a few years, recalls the eleventh duke and duchess inviting brilliant and famous friends, including Lucian Freud, during their monthlong visits. The duke was especially fond of Lismore thanks to the fishing. Some remember the duke and duchess sat on the return flight from Cork to London with baskets full of fish—the baskets were made especially for the safe transport of their prized catch. One year the duke reportedly travelled all the way home to Chatsworth with an eleven-pound salmon he caught on the River Blackwater below the castle.

Edward Sackville-West, the novelist, music critic and cousin of Vita Sackville-West, lived locally and became a regular dinner guest at the castle. Duchess Deborah recalls how, at the time, there was a craze for a game played on the billiard table called Freda, which involved running round the table at crucial moments. Sackville-West used to arrive at the door with a little case containing a change of clothes in order to save his dinner jacket from any possible damage caused by athletic undertakings during the game.

Throughout decades of sojourns to Lismore, Duchess Deborah contributed to the current aesthetic of the many rooms in the castle. The metal sign above the door into the sitting room was supposedly a favourite of hers, and when it was momentarily removed, Debo noticed immediately and instantly reinstated it—it has never been moved since. There are many porcelain chickens and floral vases propping up books along the breadth of the castle, and she undoubtedly added to the homely sense that has always been one of the most remarkable features of the gothic, imposing-looking structure. Debo added touches of chintz fabrics, such as the one on the sofa in the sitting room. This sofa needed reupholstery a few years ago, and after trialling countless fabric samples, I ended up choosing the exact same Colefax and Fowler fabric that Debo had originally chosen, now in the company's archived collection. It is often the same when any of my very

Previous pages: The dining room where works by Stephen Conroy and Peter Frie sit opposite a portrait of Elizabeth, Lady Dungarvan and Clifford, later Countess of Burlington (1613–1691) by Sir Anthony van Dyck (1599–1641); opposite: The Doctor's Bathroom with wallpaper from Cole & Son.

favourite objects need mending; I don't yet have the bravery to attempt a new look, since the current feel is so successful.

While Adele Astaire's influence upon the interior was modest, she introduced several Art Deco pieces of furniture. My mother-in-law, whose own parents were admirers of modern design, wanted to acknowledge this and pay tribute to the star who was such a feature of Lismore life in the 1930s. The queen's bathroom features an Art Deco rug and side table and a mirror-clad bath. The feel, though very different from the floral abundance of the queen's bedroom to which it is attached, is much-loved by guests for its quirkiness. Adele herself certainly had a playfulness. After her brother Fred Astaire duly signed the visitors' book after an extended visit, Adele added, 'I thought he'd never leave' below his signature. The visitors' books are treasure-troves themselves, and can be flicked through for hours on end, picking out notable names and impressive sketches by visiting artists and illustrators.

Where Adele really made her mark on Lismore was in the gardens. The tennis court that she and her husband, Lord Charles, installed still remains, but the swimming pool, which was impossibly deep, was in poor repair at the beginning of the twenty-first century. We decided to fill it in, since whenever it becomes hot enough for a dip, we choose to swim in the river. The outline of the swimming pool was intentionally preserved as a reminder of its previous history. It is interesting to observe garden visitors walking around its perimeter when in fact there is nothing to stop them from walking right over it.

The gardens have captivated each proprietor of Lismore for as long they have surrounded the castle. They are where Richard Boyle, first Earl of Cork, left a great impression of the craftsmanship of his time. The original castle walls and terraces still survive, as do the seventeenth-century gatehouse and the riding-house which acts as the bridge between the upper and lower gardens. When the sixth duke arrived for the first time to a wild and ethereal castle he observed, 'Plants grow like trees, frost is almost unknown, so myrtle, arbutus, hydrangeas, fuchsias, clianthus, erythema flourish outdoors. Salmon

Pages 54–55: The Sitting Room with sofa in a Colefax & Fowler fabric and Rosi de Ruig lampshades; pages 56–57: The lower tower bedroom with a dressing table designed by Augustus Pugin for Marlborough House, which was acquired during renovations. A portrait of Lord Richard Cavendish, son of the fourth duke, by Sir Joshua Reynolds, hangs above the bed over a Pugin patterned wallcovering by Cole & Son; opposite: The queen's bathroom was decorated by Duchess Amanda in a style inspired by Adele Astaire and hung with a collection of images of Adele dancing with her brother Fred.

to be caught under the windows almost by whistling to them'. The duke and Paxton spent time roaming the gardens, setting plans for their great projects. The eleventh duke noted in his book, *Accidents of Fortune*, that alongside fishing, the other great attraction of Lismore was the gardens. 'Gardening in Derbyshire is difficult unless you go for the hardiest of plants and shrubs. But at Lismore you can grow tender species; magnolias, rhododendrons and camellias all flourish and over the years the garden has been an ever-increasing pleasure'.

William's and my contribution to the interiors has been modest compared to those of many of our forebears. We inherited the castle in such good condition from my parents-in-law, which gave us the freedom to focus on the contemporary art gallery, the gardens and the children's literary festival. Nevertheless, on the walls and within the gardens there are reminders of our time: a photographic triptych by Ai Weiwei by the stairs, slate and mud artworks by Richard Long in the corridor, two sections of the Berlin Wall in the garden and a Franz West bench in the courtyard. My father-in-law summarises, 'There is a sense of very great age to this place. Everybody who comes here feels it. For nearly 1,400 years stones have gone up, tumbled down, been reused', which I think says it all.

Previous pages: The queen's bedroom featuring Victorian brass beds. When decorating in the early 2000s, Melissa Wyndham chose a Pugin design for the wallpaper, printed by Cole & Son. The botanical works are by Lady Emma Tennant, the twelfth duke's sister. President John F Kennedy stayed in this bedroom while visiting Lismore in 1963; opposite: Ai Weiwei's *Dropping a Han Dynasty Urn* (1995) sits above the stairs with a historical portrait of the first Earl of Cork in the background.

Spring

Irish Soda Bread

Warm Broccoli and Asparagus Salad

Marinated Pork with Peanut Sauce

Tabbouleh, Beetroot and Pomegranate

Salsa Verde

Rhubarb Amaretti Cake, Orange and Rosemary Glaze

Lemon Coconut Cloud Cake

Rhubarb Ice Cream

Opposite: Tulip pots in the upper garden with blossoms including 'Blushing Lady', 'Salmon Jimmy', 'Greenland' and 'Negrita' tulips.

The Gardens in Spring

Spring is the time to consolidate and build upon the preparation and maintenance of the dormant winter months. Firstly, we prepare the hazel hurdles and other structures for supporting peas, beans and sweet peas, as these can be readied in advance of planting when the weather warms. The vegetable plots and flowerbeds need to be prepared for the seeds or plugs to be planted once temperatures have increased. In recent years we have adopted no-dig principles in the vegetable garden at Lismore. The motivation behind this is to improve soil health and soil structure, both of which can be damaged through excess cultivation. The no-dig approach has the bonus of reducing weed pressure over time. However, we do still have to relieve the compaction of the soil that our heavy annual rainfall creates. We achieve this using a tool called a broadfork, which instead of turning and disturbing the soil, simply adds air into it, relieving any compaction. We broadfork the soil before planting the new plants and then add a layer of compost on the soil surface. We start planting seeds in trays in the polytunnels in early spring—a good inside job during what can be the bleakest time of the year. After four weeks of growing in seed trays, many plants we cultivate, such as kale, chard and celeriac, can be transferred into nine-centimetre pots. After a couple more weeks of growing, these plugs are planted in prepared beds, though onions and other *Alliaceae* can be planted straight from seed trays into the beds.

The annual addition of compost rich in nutrients and organic matter is essential to maintaining healthy soil that supports plant growth throughout the growing season. We make our own compost at Lismore, and while viewing our compost heaps is far from the most glamorous part of a visit here, they are undoubtedly important to the health of the gardens. As you enter the top of the gardens, our large heaps are in full view—a testament to the cycle of growth and production that happens within the garden's walls. All plant materials that come out of the garden are reused and split into two categories: either brown and woody, such as branches from pruning, or soft and green, including lawn cuttings. The woody material is shredded, which speeds up the breaking down of the organic materials and therefore the whole composting process. The green material can often go straight onto the compost heap. The key to a healthy and successful heap is separating out any weeds from the woody or green material and disposing of them to produce clean, organic compost.

Opposite: Hazel structures built by the garden team to support peas and beans in the vegetable garden; pages 72–73: Tulip beds in spring. Varieties grown here include 'Blushing Lady', 'La Belle Epoque', 'Vincent van Gogh', 'Salmon Impression', 'Fortress', 'Continental', 'Spring Green' and 'Francoise'; pages 80–81: Cakes in the pantry. The kitchens provide the art gallery and its café with cakes, so there is a constant supply of baked goods coming out of the pantry.

IRISH SODA BREAD

Made according to a traditional recipe, this soda bread is a Lismore Castle staple. Serve toasted with any of our jams or marmalades for breakfast, or with a good dollop of butter for any other meal. This recipe is easy to follow and is fast to make for even amateur bakers. It also makes a fantastic gift or present to a neighbour, and many of our guests take loaves home in their suitcases.

Tip: To reduce food waste, if you cannot get through a whole loaf at once just slice it up and freeze it. Take single slices out of the freezer and put straight into the toaster as needed.

Makes 2 loaves

Butter for tins

800g (6⅔ cups) whole wheat flour

75g (1¼ cups) wheat bran

75g (½ cup plus 2 tablespoons) wheat germ

100g (⅔ cup) steel-cut oatmeal

100g (¾ cup) pumpkin, sesame and sunflower seeds

2 teaspoons bicarbonate of soda

2 teaspoons fine sea salt

2 teaspoons black treacle

2 large eggs

1 litre (4 cups) buttermilk

Preheat the oven to 190°C (375°F). Butter 2 large loaf tins, line with parchment paper and set aside.

Place all the dry ingredients in a large bowl. In a medium bowl, whisk together the treacle, eggs and buttermilk. Pour this wet mixture into the dry ingredients and combine thoroughly until no dry patches remain.

Spoon into the prepared tins. Bake until a tester emerges clean, 45 to 50 minutes. Allow the loaves to cool in the tins on a rack before removing.

WARM BROCCOLI AND ASPARAGUS SALAD

This is a great recipe to use up any spare leaves or salad – don't feel limited to the leaves that we have used here. To make this dish vegan, simply swap out the anchovy for capers, and leave out the Parmesan.

Serves 8 as a main

---

2 cloves garlic, crushed

1 red chilli, seeded and chopped

4 anchovy fillets, chopped

½ teaspoon whole grain mustard

Finely grated zest and juice of 1 lemon

2 teaspoons extra virgin olive oil

Flaky sea salt and freshly ground black pepper to taste

400g (1 pound) purple sprouting broccoli

2 bunches asparagus, trimmed

Leaves of 1 head frisée

Leaves of 1 head radicchio

1 cup baby spinach

1 cup tender chard

Parmigiano Reggiano shavings for finishing

Red Onion Marmalade (page 182) for serving

To make the dressing, in a bowl combine the garlic, chilli, anchovies, mustard, zest and juice of the lemon and the olive oil. Season with salt and pepper and set aside.

Bring a large pot of water to a boil. Plunge the broccoli and asparagus into the boiling water, cook for 1 minute and then drain.

Transfer to a large bowl and spoon over the dressing. Add the frisée, radicchio, spinach and chard and toss. Top with Parmigiano and serve the marmalade on the side.

Pork and Salad

450g (1 pound) pork fillet, cut into 1-cm (½-inch) slices

1 tablespoon five spice powder

1 tablespoon nam pla or fish sauce

3 tablespoons light soy sauce

1 stalk lemongrass, finely shredded

3 red chillies, seeded and chopped

2 cloves garlic, crushed

2 shallots, finely sliced

2 tablespoons brown sugar

Sunflower oil for searing

1 handful each basil, mint and coriander leaves

1 cucumber, seeded and sliced

4 scallions

Salad for serving

50g (⅓ cup) unsalted peanuts

25g (3 tablespoons) toasted sesame seeds

-

Dressing

3 Thai red chillies, thinly sliced

1 clove garlic, crushed

3 tablespoons caster sugar

60ml (¼ cup) nam pla or fish sauce

60ml (¼ cup) lime juice

60ml (¼ cup) red wine vinegar

3 tablespoons light olive oil

MARINATED PORK WITH PEANUT SAUCE

This sticky pork remains a favourite with our guests, and while it may not be an Irish classic, it is a good showcase for garden produce. Indeed, salad and herbs are the foundation of this fresh and flavoursome dish.

Serves 4 as a main

Toss the pork fillet with the five spice powder.

Mix the nam pla, soy sauce, lemongrass, chillies, garlic, shallots and sugar in a large bowl. Add the pork, toss to coat and marinate in the refrigerator for 1 hour.

Drain the pork and reserve the marinade.

Coat a skillet large enough to hold the pork in one layer with oil and place over medium heat. Cook the pork until no longer pink, 4 to 5 minutes, then add the reserved marinade and simmer until the liquid has reduced and the pork is thoroughly cooked.

Combine the herbs, cucumber, scallions and salad. Mix the dressing ingredients together, pour over the salad and toss well. Arrange the pork on top. Garnish with the peanuts and sesame seeds and serve immediately whilst the pork is still warm.

TABBOULEH, BEETROOT AND POMEGRANATE

6 beetroots

200g (1 cup) bulghur wheat

1 cinnamon stick

100ml (¼ cup plus 2 tablespoons) extra virgin olive oil

2 tablespoons orange juice

2 teaspoons lemon juice

1 tablespoon pomegranate molasses

¼ teaspoon chilli flakes

2 cloves garlic, crushed

Salt and freshly ground black pepper to taste

1 bunch rainbow chard, stems and leaves sliced

¼ head red cabbage, cored and thinly sliced

6 scallions, thinly sliced

Seeds and juice of 1 pomegranate

1 bunch rocket (arugula)

25g (3 tablespoons) pumpkin seeds, toasted

25g (3 tablespoons) pine nuts, toasted

Leaves of 1 bunch basil, torn

Leaves of 1 bunch coriander, chopped

2 oranges, peeled and segmented

This dish can be served as a main course, perhaps topped off with some fried halloumi, or as a side dish with a BBQ or roast chicken, depending on the spring weather. If you don't have bulghur wheat in your pantry then you can swap it out for pearl barley or quinoa.

Serves 6 as a side dish

Preheat the oven to 200°C (400°F). Wrap the beetroots individually in foil and roast until tender. Allow to cool, then peel, halve and cut into thin wedges. Place the beets in a large bowl.

Put the bulghur in a saucepan with the cinnamon and 15ml (1 tablespoon) olive oil. Add 250ml (1 cup) of water. Bring to a boil, cover and remove from the heat. Allow to rest for 30 minutes. Remove the lid, remove and discard cinnamon stick and fluff bulghur with a fork, then allow to cool completely.

To make the dressing, whisk together the juices, molasses, remaining olive oil, chilli and garlic. Season with salt and pepper.

Add the chard and cabbage to the beets and dress with some of the dressing. Toss and allow to rest for 30 minutes. Add the bulghur to the beets, dress and toss to combine. Add the scallions and pomegranate seeds and juice. Taste and adjust dressing and seasoning. Transfer to a serving bowl and top with rocket, pumpkin seeds, pine nuts, herbs and oranges.

SALSA VERDE

This sauce is quick and fresh and works with several of the recipes in this book. It is often a companion to our Tabbouleh, Beetroot and Pomegranate (page 77), Rainbow Chard, Tomato and Parmesan (page 98) and Spring Pea, Broad Bean and Goat's Cheese Salad (page 107), but can be served with any grilled fish, meats or salads. You can make it in advance, and it will stay fresh in a kilner jar in the fridge for a week. Allow it to come to room temperature before you serve it.

Serves 6

Leaves of 2 large bunches parsley

Leaves of 2 large bunches basil

Leaves of 2 large bunches mint

3 cloves garlic, peeled and crushed

2 tablespoons capers

4 anchovy fillets

1 tablespoon Dijon mustard

Juice of 2 lemons

120ml (½ cup) extra virgin olive oil

Salt and freshly ground black pepper to taste

Place all the ingredients in a food processor fitted with the metal blade and process until smooth.

Taste and adjust seasoning.

RHUBARB AMARETTI CAKE, ORANGE AND ROSEMARY GLAZE

Rhubarb harvests are famously bountiful, so we look for creative ways to use this delicious and versatile vegetable. When it is combined with sweet amaretti, zesty orange and earthy rosemary, the result is this impressive cake, which is also a feast for the eyes.

Cake

225g (2 sticks) unsalted butter, softened

200g (1 cup) golden caster (raw) sugar

1 teaspoon vanilla extract

4 large eggs

Grated zest of 2 oranges

200g (2 cups) almonds, ground

50g (¼ cup plus 2 tablespoons) plain (all-purpose) flour

1 teaspoon baking power

8 amaretti biscuits, broken into small chunks

3 stalks rhubarb, halved lengthwise and cut into 6-cm (2½-inch) pieces

-

Glaze

Juice of 1 orange

1 sprig rosemary

20g (2 tablespoons) granulated sugar

2 teaspoons lemon juice

Serves 8

Preheat the oven to 180°C (350°F) and line the bottom of a 23-cm (9-inch) tart tin with a removable bottom with parchment.

For the cake, beat the butter and sugar in an electric mixer until light and fluffy. Add the vanilla extract. Add the eggs one at a time, beating to incorporate between additions. Fold in the orange zest, ground almonds, flour, baking powder and amaretti biscuit pieces. Pour the mixture into the prepared tin and smooth the top with a spatula. Gently push the rhubarb pieces into the batter in a spoke pattern. Bake until golden, 30 to 40 minutes.

Allow to cool in the tin for 10 minutes, then lift out and cool completely on a wire rack.

For the glaze, combine the orange juice, rosemary and sugar in a heavy saucepan and bring to a simmer. Simmer briskly for 5 minutes to reduce the liquid slightly, then remove from the heat. Stir in the lemon juice. Remove and discard rosemary. Allow the glaze to cool slightly, then pour warm glaze over the cooled cake.

LEMON COCONUT CLOUD CAKE

This recipe is for a light and airy sponge with an indulgent frosting. The coconut and lemon combination makes for an unusual twist on a classic lemon cake. We decorate ours with edible flowers if they are in season, or just a dusting of coconut flakes if they are not.

Serves 8 to 10

Layers

100g (7 tablespoons) unsalted butter, plus more for tin

300g (2½ cups) plain (all-purpose) flour

1 teaspoon baking powder

1 teaspoon bicarbonate of soda

300g (1½ cups) caster sugar

250g (1 cup) coconut milk

1 tablespoon coconut oil

1 teaspoon vanilla extract

2 large eggs

200ml (¾ cup plus 2 tablespoons) sunflower oil

Juice of 1 lemon

-

Icing

200g (1 stick plus 6 tablespoons) unsalted butter, softened

250g (2 cups) icing sugar

Finely grated zest and juice of 1 lemon

1 teaspoon coconut oil

Coconut flakes or edible flowers for finishing

To make the layers, preheat the oven to 170°C (325°F). Butter two round 20-cm (8-inch) springform tins and line the bottoms with parchment paper.

In a bowl, sift together the flour, baking powder, bicarbonate and sugar. Place the 100g (7 tablespoons) of butter, coconut milk and coconut oil in a saucepan and place over low heat until the butter has melted. In a bowl, whisk together the vanilla, eggs, sunflower oil and lemon juice.

Add the butter mixture to the flour and other dry ingredients and stir well. Then add the egg mixture and combine to form a smooth batter. Divide the batter between the tins and bake until golden and a tester in the centre emerges clean, 30 to 40 minutes. Cool the cakes in their tins on a wire rack.

While the cakes cool, make the icing. Combine the butter, sugar, lemon zest and juice and coconut oil in an electric mixer and beat until smooth and fluffy.

When the cakes have completely cooled, remove from their tins. Overturn them so the flat sides are facing up and peel off the parchment. Place one layer on a cake plate and frost the top. Top with the second layer and frost the top and sides with the remaining icing. Scatter on coconut flakes or add flowers.

RHUBARB ICE CREAM

This recipe was born from looking at new ways to use this delicious vegetable. The cream and sugar soften the rhubarb's tart quality, and we serve this with a small shortbread on the side for the perfect dessert.

Makes 4 pints

500ml (2 cups) cream

150ml (½ cup plus 2 tablespoons) milk

1 vanilla pod split lengthways, seeds scraped and pod reserved

8 egg yolks

330g (1½ cups plus 2 tablespoons) caster sugar

1kg (2¼ pounds) rhubarb, trimmed and cut into 5-cm (2-inch) chunks

In a saucepan, combine the cream and milk and place over low heat. Add the vanilla seeds and slowly bring to a boil. When the mixture begins to bubble, remove it from the heat and set aside to infuse for 30 minutes.

Meanwhile, beat the egg yolks with 150g (¾ cup) of the sugar until thick and pale. Gently reheat the cream mixture and add it to the egg mixture in a thin stream, whisking constantly.

Transfer the mixture to a clean saucepan and cook over very low heat until the custard thickens and coats the back of a spoon. Remove from the heat, transfer to a clean bowl and allow to cool completely.

Place the rhubarb in a saucepan with 250ml (1 cup) water, the vanilla pod and the remaining 180g (¾ cup plus 2 tablespoons) sugar. Bring to a simmer over low heat and cook until the rhubarb is soft but still intact, 6 to 7 minutes.

Strain the rhubarb and reserve the liquid. Place the rhubarb in a heatproof bowl. Transfer the liquid to a small saucepan and return to the heat. Simmer until reduced by half. Pour over the rhubarb and allow to cool.

Pour the cooled custard into an ice cream maker and churn according to manufacturer's instructions until thickened but not set. Add the rhubarb and churn for 10 additional minutes. Alternatively, transfer the mixture to a container and place it in the freezer. After 1 hour, remove the mixture and stir and break it up. Repeat two more times, waiting 1 hour in between, then allow to freeze completely.

Summer

Rainbow Chard, Tomato and Parmesan

Beetroot Gravadlax

Cucumber and Fennel Salad

Spring Pea, Broad Bean and Goat's Cheese Salad

Fennel, Tomato and Burrata Salad

Buttermilk Rosemary Focaccia

Gooseberry and Elderflower Sorbet

Lemon Rosemary Squares

Summer Berry Tiramisù

Previous pages: The old cut-flower border. Flowers seen include *Digitalis purpurea, Daucus carota, Dipsacus fullonum, Euphorbia corallioides, Thalictrum* 'Elin' and *Lupinus polyphyllus*. The apple trees are all *Malus domestica*; opposite: Perennials growing in front of the castle include *Verbascum chaixii, Sanguisorba officinalis* 'Pink Tanna', *Stipa gigantea, Echium pininana, Baptisia australis, Malus domestica, Cordyline australis* and *Acacia dealbata*.

The Gardens in Summer

While each season comes with its own long job list, during summer there is no time to sit down and plan or set to tidying sheds or tools since every minute is needed in the thick of the gardens. When the weather warms, it is the moment to directly sow the seeds of vegetables that prefer to go straight into the ground, since their roots do not like the disturbance of being moved once they have begun to grow—beetroot, carrots and peas are prime examples. At the same time, the plugs that were planted during spring as seeds in the polytunnels are planted in the vegetable beds. However, it is important to wait until the soil is dry enough, as the seeds will quickly rot in waterlogged ground. These crops then need regular attention for the rest of the summer, whether it be hoeing between the plants to get rid of weeds or regular watering during dry spells. The fruit bushes need picking throughout the later summer months. We keep all our berries in fruit cages to protect the crop from scavenging wildlife.

In high summer, even when the castle is full of guests, the supply from the gardens outweighs the demand from the kitchen. Any surplus produce is sold at a stand near the garden entrance.

The rest of the garden demands much attention as well. Flowerbeds and borders need to be weeded and hoed by hand. Weeds are inevitable, especially since we do not spray any chemicals in the garden, and while we keep on top of the worst of it, we see weeds as part of the ecosystem and do not eradicate them altogether. We leave the orchard meadow untouched altogether to allow the wildflowers and oxeye daisies to flourish amongst the grass.

Opposite: Cold-frames full of lettuce ready for harvest. The red is the Lollo Rossa 'Matador'. The green is the endive 'Can Can'; following pages: Paxton's vinery, the last surviving Paxton greenhouse in Ireland.

Paxton's Vinery

The vinery pictured on the previous page was constructed around 1853 under the design and direction of Joseph Paxton as part of the sixth Duke of Devonshire's renovations. It originally consisted of a twelve-bay glass structure. However, the last four bays to the east were later removed, possibly during the early twentieth century. The vinery was conceived to grow grapevines and incorporates a ridge and furrow design, a system which sets the glass at right angles to both the morning and evening sun, maximising the availability of light and heat. One vine per ridge and furrow bay was trained from its planting place outside the vinery, through the square openings on the south-facing wall and up the centre of each ridge. The roots of grapevines benefit from being exposed to winter chill, which is why they are planted outside the vinery.

A vinery was traditionally equipped with a boiler and cast-iron heating pipes to guarantee the growth of vines and other plants. At Lismore these no longer exist. They likely were removed at the same time as the last four bays; a single remaining cast-iron floor grid located in front of the east entrance testifies to their former existence. As for the original vine, it was destroyed by an insect pest in the late nineteenth century and has subsequently been replaced with one cultivated at Chatsworth.

Internally, the vinery originally hosted two large, raised planting beds parted by a concrete footpath. The footpath was connected to the potting shed at the rear by a short flight of steps. No traces of the original floor remain, although vineries of this date typically had terracotta tiles such as those currently present. The heating system was fitted in the original Paxton design, but it's doubtful that the vinery would have been used to grow tropical plants. Rather the heat was in place to force vines into early growth in spring and to aid fruit ripening as the weather cooled in the autumn. Although the original purpose of the vinery would have been purely productive, the present-day planting is a mixture of production and ornamental display.

Restoration

The vinery is a building of national importance and is believed to be the only surviving example of Paxton's ridge and furrow system in Ireland. Therefore, bringing it back from the poor condition into which it had gradually slipped over time was essential, and works to restore the vinery began in 2018.

The restoration was undertaken with the intent of retaining as much of the historical fabric as possible. Approximately 60 percent of the original roof glazing bars were retained, with new ends and new tongues grafted onto the sound historical timber. Likewise, around 95 percent of the ironmongery and original sash-opening mechanisms were repaired and reinstated. The timber used for the repairs was accoya, a sustainably grown softwood treated with a process called acetylation, which alters the structure of the wood and ensures dimensional stability and exceptional durability. The first five bays were kept for growing vines to maintain historical context. Restoration work was completed in 2022.

The vinery in its present incarnation is an unheated glasshouse, meaning that the plants grown within still need to have a modicum of hardiness to survive the lower temperatures of winter. With this in mind, the garden team decided the best-suited ornamental planting would be Mediterranean-climate plants, many of which survive low temperatures so long as their roots are dry. The gardeners can control watering, and it is kept to an absolute minimum during winter. As with all gardens, though, planting will evolve and change over time. Having such a large area under glass is an asset to any garden and a gift for any horticulturalist.

Pages 104–5: A pergola built from a fallen chestnut tree on the estate has a mix of climbers, including 'The Generous Gardener' roses, *Actinidia deliciosa* 'Solissimo' and *Vitis vinifera*; pages 110–11: A wildflower mix of flora such as oxeye daises under the historical apple trees; pages 116–17: Walls clad with a climbing rose and *Centranthus ruber* (red valerian). Also seen are *Melanoselinum decipiens* (black parsley) and *Yucca filamentosa*. Ithuriel's spear (*Triteleia laxa*) and *Euphorbia corallioides* among foxglove (*Digitalis purpurea*), wild carrot (*Daucus carota*), giant hog fennel (*Peucedanum verticillare*) and delphiniums; pages 122–23: Early morning in the upper garden, featuring *Achillea millefolium* 'Moonshine', the umbellifer *Selinum wallichianum*, soft pink *Althea cannabina*, golden oat grass (*Stipa gigantea*) and *Sanguisorba officinalis* 'Pink Tanna'.

RAINBOW CHARD, TOMATO AND PARMESAN

This is the perfect salad, adaptable for using what is readily available in the garden. It is highly flexible, and you can exchange fruits and vegetables as the seasons progress. We serve this dish for breakfast with eggs, as a light lunch with Warm Broccoli and Asparagus Salad (page 71) or as a side dish to meat and fish later in the day.

Serves 8

Olive oil for sautéing

2 red onions, sliced

2 leeks, sliced

4 cloves garlic, sliced

Freshly grated nutmeg to taste

Sea salt and freshly ground black pepper to taste

Red chilli flakes to taste

2 bay leaves

500g (1 pound) rainbow chard, trimmed, stalks and leaves separated and chopped into 5-cm (2-inch) pieces

6 large tomatoes, diced

50g (¼ cup) green olives, pitted

Finely grated zest and juice of 1 lemon

Grated and shaved Parmigiano Reggiano for finishing

Torn fresh oregano and basil leaves for finishing

Place a large skillet over low heat with olive oil and sauté the red onions and leeks until soft and golden. Add the garlic and season with nutmeg, salt and pepper and chilli flakes. Stir in bay leaves.

Add the chard leaves and stalks and cook, stirring occasionally, until wilted. Add the tomatoes and cook until they soften. Add the olives, lemon zest and juice and season to taste, then remove from the heat. Remove and discard bay leaves. Fold in grated Parmigiano.

Transfer the dish to a serving bowl and top with Parmigiano shavings and torn herbs.

BEETROOT GRAVADLAX

1 full side salmon, skin on and pin-boned

3 tablespoons flaky sea salt

1 tablespoon freshly ground black pepper

3 tablespoons caster sugar

3 tablespoons chopped fresh dill

6 juniper berries, crushed

1 teaspoon freshly grated horseradish

One 300-g (11-ounce) beetroot, peeled and coarsely grated

Zest of 2 lemons

50ml (3 tablespoons) gin

-

Mustard and Dill Sauce

2 teaspoons whole-grain mustard

200ml (¾ cup) sour cream

Finely grated zest and juice of 1 lemon

Chopped fresh dill to taste

Sea salt and freshly ground black pepper

Salmon fishing from the banks of the River Blackwater has been a pastime for as long as the castle has stood above the river. The best way to honour this tradition is with an impressive full side of salmon centre-stage at a large gathering. Serve with the mustard and dill sauce below, or with Cucumber and Fennel Salad (page 103). Since this dish is prepared two days before it is consumed, it is ideal for buffets and lunches where you want to enjoy your guests and not worry about what is in the oven.

Serves 10 as a starter

Place the salmon on a large tray or platter, skin side down. Mix the salt, pepper, sugar, dill, juniper berries and horseradish. Spread the mixture all over the salmon so that the flesh is completely covered. Scatter the beetroot and lemon zest on top. Drizzle with the gin.

Cover the tray as tightly as possible with clingfilm. Place a weight on top, such as another tray, to help pack everything down. Refrigerate for 48 hours.

Remove the clingfilm and pour off the liquid from the tray. Wipe away all the toppings and pat dry with kitchen paper.

To serve, thinly slice with a sharp knife.

For the Mustard and Dill Sauce, mix all the ingredients together and adjust seasoning to taste.

CUCUMBER AND FENNEL SALAD

This zesty dish is a great accompaniment to the Beetroot Gravadlax on page 100. With equally sharp colours and packed full of fresh flavours, the two go hand-in-hand. It is worth investing in a hand-held julienne peeler to speed up the vegetable preparation.

Serves 6 as a side dish

---

1 tablespoon white wine vinegar

1 teaspoon caster sugar

1 tablespoon extra virgin olive oil

Juice of 1 lemon

Sea salt and freshly ground black pepper to taste

1 tablespoon chopped fresh dill

1 tablespoon chopped fresh parsley

½ red chilli, finely diced

1 cucumber, seeded and sliced

1 red onion, sliced

4 radishes, quartered

1 bulb fennel, cored, quartered and sliced

2 carrots, peeled and cut into ribbons

Combine the vinegar, sugar, oil and lemon juice to make dressing. Season to taste and stir in herbs and chilli.

In a serving bowl, combine the cucumber, onion, radishes, fennel and carrots. Dress and toss to combine.

SPRING PEA, BROAD BEAN AND GOAT'S CHEESE SALAD

Fresh garden peas—picked, podded and eaten on the same day—are hard to beat. If you do not have access to these, use frozen peas but blanch them only for 1 minute. This salad combines various beans and peas and is the taste of summer. If weather permits, this recipe is ideal for outside dining and picnicking.

Serves 8 as a main

300g (11 ounces) fresh broad (fava) beans, podded

Sea salt to taste

300g (11 ounces) fresh peas, podded

100g (4 ounces) green beans

8 slices pancetta

150g (5 ounces) soft goat's cheese

1 clove garlic, pounded

Freshly ground black pepper to taste

2 teaspoons runny honey

Juice of 1 lemon

2 tablespoons light olive oil, plus more for drizzling

Leaves of 1 large bunch fresh mint, finely chopped

Preheat the oven to 200°C (400°F).

Blanch the broad (fava) beans in boiling salted water for 1 minute, drain and refresh in ice water. Drain and remove and discard the skins.

Blanch the peas and green beans in salted boiling water until just tender. Drain, refresh in ice water and drain again.

Place the pancetta in a single layer on a baking tray and bake until crispy, about 10 minutes.

Meanwhile, in a bowl combine the goat's cheese and garlic and season with salt and pepper, then stir in the honey and lemon juice.

In a serving bowl, toss the beans and peas with the 2 tablespoons olive oil. Sprinkle on the chopped mint and the cheese mixture. Crumble the pancetta and add to the salad. Drizzle with oil and serve.

FENNEL, TOMATO AND BURRATA SALAD

At Lismore, we grow several varieties of fennel. Our favourite for this salad is Florence fennel. It has a short season which usually coincides with the time when the tomatoes are in their prime. Any type of mozzarella can also be used in the salad, but extra-creamy burrata is our favourite.

Serves 8 as a main

2 bulbs fennel, cored and thinly sliced

2 red onions, thinly sliced

1 bunch radishes, halved and sliced

400g (1 pound) mixed cherry and plum tomatoes, sliced, halved or quartered

2 cucumbers, thinly sliced

120ml (½ cup) extra virgin olive oil

60ml (¼ cup) red wine vinegar

Sea salt and freshly ground black pepper to taste

Juice of 1 orange

Juice of 1 lemon

1 red chilli, seeded and chopped

3 cloves garlic, crushed

6 clementines, peeled and segmented

8 small balls burrata, 75g (3 ounces) each

Chopped fresh oregano and dill for garnish

Toasted pine nuts and pistachios for garnish

In a large bowl combine the fennel, onions, radishes, tomatoes and cucumbers. In a small bowl whisk together the oil and vinegar. Season and add the juices. Stir in the chilli and garlic. Taste and adjust seasoning as required.

Dress the salad with some of the dressing, then add the clementines. Toss and transfer to a serving bowl. Top with the burrata. Sprinkle with chopped herbs and nuts. Drizzle on the remaining dressing.

BUTTERMILK ROSEMARY FOCACCIA

Focaccia can be made and enjoyed year-round, but we especially like to serve it alongside our summer salads in this chapter. It has a lightness and saltiness that works particularly well in summer.

Makes one 23-cm by 23-cm (9-inch by 9-inch) focaccia

450g (3¾ cups) plain (all-purpose) flour, plus more for work surface

1 teaspoon fine sea salt

1 teaspoon bicarbonate of soda

400ml (1⅔ cups) buttermilk

Olive oil for tin and drizzling

Flaky sea salt to taste

Rosemary for topping

Preheat the oven on fan/convection to 180°C (350°F).

Sift the 450g (3¾ cups) flour, fine salt and bicarbonate of soda into a large mixing bowl. Add the buttermilk in a thin stream while stirring with a wooden spoon. Knead by hand in the bowl to form a soft dough.

Place the dough on a lightly floured surface and shape into a rough square.

Oil a 23-cm (9-inch) square baking tin. Transfer the dough to the tin. Press with your fingertips to dimple the dough. Drizzle olive oil generously over the surface of the dough. Sprinkle with the flaky salt and rosemary.

Bake until golden brown, about 30 minutes. Serve warm.

GOOSEBERRY AND ELDERFLOWER SORBET

We have elderflower in abundance at Lismore. We pick it from late May for a few weeks. In addition to making Elderflower Cordial (page 212), we love this sorbet as the ultimate refresher on warm summer days—which we have plenty of in Ireland, to the surprise of some. For the best flavour, pick elderflower on a dry day, not during the rain.

Serves 8 to 10

1kg (2¼ pounds) gooseberries

5 elderflower heads

225g (1 cup plus 2 tablespoons) caster sugar

Finely grated zest and juice of 4 lemons

Poach the gooseberries and elderflower heads in a little water until soft. Take out the elderflower heads and reserve. Force the rest of the mixture through a sieve.

Dissolve the sugar in 600ml (2½ cups) of water and boil briskly for 6 to 8 minutes to make a light syrup. Remove from the heat and add the elderflowers and lemon juice and zest. Allow to cool, then strain and add to the gooseberries.

Pour into an ice cream maker and churn according to manufacturer's instructions for 20 minutes. Alternatively, transfer the mixture to a container and place it in the freezer. After 2 hours, remove the mixture and stir and break it up. Repeat two more times, waiting 2 hours in between, then allow to freeze completely. Before serving, take out of the freezer and refrigerate for 30 minutes.

LEMON ROSEMARY SQUARES

These cake squares are always popular. It is useful to have a few pre-prepared at busy times, as they go with anything, at any time of day—perhaps a treat snuck into a picnic or served with afternoon tea. They are a pleasant combination of tart lemon and sugar, just sweet enough but not too much.

Makes 12 squares

Cake

250g (1 stick plus 6 tablespoons) unsalted butter, softened, plus more for tin

250g (1¼ cups) caster sugar

250g (2 cups) self-rising flour

3 large eggs

-

Glaze

175g (¾ cup plus 2 tablespoons) caster sugar

Finely grated zest and juice of 2 lemons

2 tablespoons chopped rosemary

For the cake, preheat the oven on fan/convection to 180°C (350°F). Line a shallow tin measuring 20 cm by 25 cm (8 inches by 10 inches) with parchment and butter the parchment.

In a food processor fitted with the metal blade, combine the 250g (1 stick plus 6 tablespoons) butter, sugar and flour. Process until smooth. Pour into the prepared pan. Bake until well risen and golden brown, about 20 minutes.

While the cake is baking, prepare the glaze. Mix the sugar with the lemon zest and juice until smooth, then stir in the chopped rosemary.

As soon as the cake is baked, pour the glaze over the top. Allow to cool completely before cutting into squares.

SUMMER BERRY TIRAMISÙ

This pudding is a fresh twist on the classic Italian recipe and contains no coffee, making it an ideal dessert for young and old when the berries are in season.

Serves 8

250g (1¼ cups) caster sugar

175g (6 ounces - ½ pint basket) strawberries

175g (6 ounces - ½ pint basket) blueberries

175g (6 ounces - ½ pint basket) raspberries

2 tablespoons crème de cassis

3 large eggs, separated

400g (1⅔ cups) mascarpone

1 tablespoon vanilla extract

40 savoiardi biscuits

50g (⅓ cup) toasted hazelnuts, chopped

50g (2 ounces) dark chocolate shavings

In a saucepan, combine 150ml (½ cup plus 2 tablespoons) water with 110g (½ cup) of the sugar until dissolved, then simmer to make a light syrup. Add the fruit and poach gently for 2 minutes. Strain the fruit and reserve the syrup and the fruit separately.

Combine the syrup and the cassis.

In a separate bowl, whisk the egg yolks with the remaining 140g (¾ cup) sugar until pale. Whisk in the mascarpone and vanilla.

In a third bowl, beat the egg whites to stiff peaks, then fold them into the mascarpone mixture.

Dip half the biscuits in the syrup and line the bottom of a square serving dish with them. Spread half the egg mixture over the biscuits, then scatter half of the fruit on top. Repeat with the remaining biscuits, fruit and egg mixture.

Cover and refrigerate for at least 8 hours. Finish with toasted hazelnuts and chocolate shavings just before serving.

Autumn

Breakfast Granola

Ruby Chard, Squash, Feta Filo Tart

Autumn Salad

Baked Figs with Gorgonzola and Walnuts

Tuscan Kale, Borlotti Bean and Courgette Casserole

Spiced Cauliflower and Potatoes

Fresh Fig Tart

Courgette Walnut Cake

Caramel Custards with Baked Pears and Bay

Opposite: The lower garden with a variety of different Japanese maples: 'Inaba-shidare', 'Katsura', 'Seiryu' and 'Skeeter's Broom'; page 127: Colm O'Driscoll, head gardener, picks apples in the upper garden.

The Gardens in Autumn

The gardens still produce through the early autumn months thanks to the mild temperatures and ample rainfall of the Irish climate. This means we can keep the kitchen stocked with fresh produce for much of the year. In these months, the orchard in the upper garden comes into its own and the garden team turn their attention to harvesting apples for a few days. The apples are then used to produce the apple juice sold in the gallery shop (see page 211 for more on our juice). Since we are prone to wet winters in Ireland, it is important that we protect the soil to keep the lashings of rain from eroding the surface and leaching the soil of nutrients. The soil is happiest when it has roots planted in it, and this is why we plant green manure cover crops to protect the soil over the winter months. These are fast-growing plants such as crimson clover (*Trifolium incarnatum*), *Phacelia tanacetifolia*, winter vetch (*Vicia villosa*) and rye, which we sow in early September. These plants establish quickly and mop up any nutrients left in the beds from the summer's crops. They also provide a layer of protection for the soil over the winter months, reducing erosion and supporting the life below the soil. They are mulched down in early spring and left on the soil surface to decompose back into the soil. This helps feed the soil and ensures that it is healthy and ready for planting. If beds become empty beyond October, we usually choose to mulch the soil with compost instead of planting green manure.

Storing Vegetables

Historically, we have stored many root vegetables through the winter; however, with the success of the vegetable sales at the garden gate, we are finding less of a need to do this. Nevertheless, it is a useful tool to avoid waste and continue supply of quality homegrown vegetables throughout the sparser months of the year. Here is our simple guide to storing root vegetables:

- Line the bottom of a crate, pallet or container with a compost bag or reuse any large sheets of plastic you might have.
- Add compost or wood chips to cover the bottom of the sheet.
- Prepare the vegetable by twisting off their tops (we do this rather than cutting, as the sap can bleed out when vegetables are sliced by a blade). Keep to one type of vegetable per crate.
- Add a single layer of the vegetables, cover fully with compost or wood chips, place in a cool dark space and repeat until all your vegetables are safe for their winter hibernation.

BREAKFAST GRANOLA

You can use whatever nuts and seeds you have available for this granola. We like to use pecans, almonds and hazelnuts and sesame, pumpkin and sunflower seeds. Our favourite way to serve this granola is by sprinkling a good handful over natural yoghurt with seasonal fresh fruits from the garden. This cereal will keep for two months if you store it in an airtight kilner jar.

Makes 2 medium jars

300g (3 cups) rolled oats

150g (1¼ cups) mixed nuts and seeds

60ml (¼ cup) maple syrup

60ml (¼ cup) light olive oil

100g (½ cup) brown sugar

Pinch flaky sea salt

Preheat the oven to 150°C (300°F).

Combine the oats and nuts and seeds in a bowl.

Combine the maple syrup, oil and sugar in a saucepan and cook, stirring, over medium heat until the sugar dissolves. Add to the oats and nuts and mix well.

Scatter the mixture on a large baking tray in a thin layer. Bake, stirring every 5 minutes to keep from burning, until golden brown, about 40 minutes.

Allow the granola to cool completely, then break up the large chunks to your preferred size.

RUBY CHARD, SQUASH, FETA FILO TART

Chard can be found throughout late summer and autumn. The ruby variety adds visual punch to this dish with its vibrantly coloured stems. Autumn chard has a stronger taste and is more robust than that picked in summer. We serve this with our Autumn Salad (page 135) or a simple green leaf salad with a little shaved manchego or Parmesan on top.

Makes one 24-cm ($9\frac{1}{2}$-inch) tart, serves 6 to 8

Extra virgin olive oil for tin, sautéing and drizzling

2 red onions, finely chopped

2 cloves garlic, peeled and crushed

1 butternut squash, peeled, seeded and diced

3 eggs, beaten

100g (1 cup) grated Parmigiano Reggiano

Sea salt and freshly ground black pepper to taste

½ teaspoon coriander seeds, toasted and ground

¼ teaspoon cumin seeds, toasted and ground

¼ teaspoon ground turmeric

Coriander and basil leaves to taste

150g (5 ounces) ruby chard, cut into ribbons

100g (4 ounces) chargrilled red pepper, cut into strips

Finely grated zest and juice of 1 lemon

200g (7 ounces) filo dough

100g (⅔ cup) crumbled feta

In a large skillet, sauté the onions in olive oil over low heat for 5 minutes. Add the garlic and the squash and cook, stirring occasionally, until the squash has begun to soften, about 10 minutes.

Transfer to a bowl and add the beaten eggs and grated Parmigiano. Season with salt and pepper and stir in the ground coriander, cumin and turmeric. Add the herbs.

In a separate bowl toss the chard and red pepper with the lemon juice and zest and drizzle with a little olive oil.

Line the tin with the filo, allowing the extra to hang over the edges. Drizzle the pastry with a little oil and arrange the squash mixture in an even layer across the base of the tin. Scatter the chard and peppers on top and the feta on top of those.

Fold the excess filo back over the filling around the perimeter. Bake on the bottom shelf of the oven for 30 minutes. Allow to cool in the tin on a rack for 5 minutes before removing the tart.

AUTUMN SALAD

Dressing

2 egg yolks

1 teaspoon Dijon mustard

1 tablespoon cider vinegar

1 tablespoon cream

1 tablespoon honey

1 teaspoon pomegranate molasses

Juice of 1 lemon

200ml (¾ cup plus 2 tablespoons) mild olive oil

-

Salad

½ head red cabbage, cored and cut into very thin ribbons

3 beetroots, peeled and thinly sliced

2 bulbs fennel, trimmed and thinly sliced

3 carrots, peeled and shaved with a peeler

3 sweet apples, cored and sliced

2 pink grapefruits, peeled and segmented

1 small bunch tarragon, chopped

50g (⅓ cup) roughly chopped toasted hazelnuts

25g (3 tablespoons) sunflower seeds, toasted

Seeds of 1 pomegranate

Beetroot, cabbage, carrots and apple make this dish burst with colour. It is a reminder that the growing season is not over yet, and there is plenty more produce still to be enjoyed from the garden.

Serves 6 to 8 as a side dish

To make the dressing put the egg yolks in a bowl. Add the mustard, cider vinegar and cream and whisk to combine. Stir in the honey, molasses and lemon juice. Add the oil in a thin stream, whisking constantly.

In a large serving bowl, combine the cabbage, beetroots, fennel, carrots, apples, grapefruits and tarragon. Drizzle with dressing and toss to combine. Scatter on the nuts, seeds and pomegranate and serve.

BAKED FIGS WITH GORGONZOLA AND WALNUTS

The figs in our gardens are usually ready beginning in August. Interestingly, figs grown in our Irish climate actually develop over two seasons: in late autumn, the gardeners inspect the fig trees to identify young fruits that are growing on the branches that are smaller than a thumbnail. These are the fruits that will overwinter and then develop into ripe figs the following summer. Anything larger than a thumbnail is unlikely to ripen that season and is prone to rotting. We therefore remove this fruit to conserve the fig trees' energy and funnel it into the fruit which will ripen the following season. We serve this dish as a starter, but it makes an equally delicious light supper or lunch with a slice of Irish Soda Bread (page 69).

Serves 4 as a starter

---

8 ripe figs, stemmed

150g (5 ounces) Gorgonzola

200g (1⅔ cups) toasted walnuts, chopped

1 teaspoon honey

1 teaspoon balsamic vinegar

2 tablespoons extra virgin olive oil

Preheat the oven to 180°C (350°F).

Cut an X into each fig, leaving 2 cm (¾ inch) at the bottom intact. Squeeze the centres to open the figs a little and place the figs in an ovenproof dish.

Mix the Gorgonzola and walnuts. Fill the figs with the Gorgonzola mixture. Combine the honey, vinegar and oil in a small saucepan and warm over low heat, then drizzle over the figs.

Bake for 6 minutes and serve warm.

TUSCAN KALE, BORLOTTI BEAN AND COURGETTE CASSEROLE

200g (1 cup) dried borlotti beans, soaked overnight and drained

Sea salt to taste

2 bay leaves

Freshly ground black pepper to taste

Extra virgin olive oil for drizzling and sautéing

4 strips pancetta, chopped

2 red onions, sliced

2 carrots, peeled and diced

4 cloves garlic, thinly sliced

1 bulb fennel, trimmed and sliced

Leaves and stems of 1 large bunch basil, kept separate and coarsely chopped

2 ribs celery, chopped

800g (1¾ pounds) plum tomatoes, seeded and chopped

1 glass (½ cup) red wine

1 potato, peeled and diced

2 courgettes (zucchini), sliced

200g (7 ounces) Tuscan kale, cut into ribbons

50g (¼ cup) orzo

Parmigiano Reggiano shavings for finishing

As autumn progresses and the sky turns dark earlier, we naturally change what we eat and serve. Led by the garden, we combine the last of the summer produce to create this comforting dish packed with vegetables.

Serves 8 as a main

Cook the drained beans in salted boiling water with the bay leaves until tender. Remove and discard bay leaves. Reserve 240ml (1 cup) cooking liquid. Drain the beans. Season with salt and black pepper and drizzle with a little olive oil.

Heat a little olive oil in a saucepan and add the chopped pancetta, onions, carrots, garlic, fennel, basil stems and celery. Cook, covered and stirring occasionally, over low heat until softened but not browned, about 15 minutes.

Add the tomatoes, red wine and potato and simmer for 15 additional minutes. Add the courgettes (zucchini), kale, the reserved 240ml (1 cup) cooking liquid and beans and the orzo. Cook, stirring frequently, until the orzo is tender. If the mixture seems too thick, add water in small amounts.

Taste and adjust seasoning and sprinkle with the basil leaves. Drizzle with olive oil and top with Parmigiano shavings and serve.

SPICED CAULIFLOWER AND POTATOES

This recipe works well as a vegetarian main dish or can be served as a side with almost any of the dishes in the book. If you follow our tips for storing vegetables on page 126 and store cauliflower and squash, you can serve it with the Spiced Squash Tagine (page 158).

Serves 6 as a main

3 large onions, thinly sliced

Sunflower oil for sautéing

4 cloves garlic, peeled and crushed

One 3-cm (1¼-inch) piece of ginger, peeled and minced

1 tablespoon ground coriander

2 teaspoons ground cumin

½ teaspoon cayenne pepper

½ teaspoon ground turmeric

4 medium tomatoes, chopped

Sea salt and freshly ground black pepper to taste

3 potatoes, peeled and cut into large chunks

1 large head cauliflower, broken into large florets

100g (⅔ cups) cashews, toasted

Seeds of 6 cardamom pods, ground

1 tablespoon garam masala

180g (¾ cup) crème fraiche

Leaves of 1 bunch coriander

In a large pot, sauté 1 onion in a little oil over medium heat. Add the garlic and continue to cook until softened. Add the ginger and stir in the ground coriander, cumin, cayenne and turmeric. Sauté for another 2 minutes. Add the chopped tomatoes and 500ml (2 cups) of water. Season with salt and pepper.

Bring the mixture to a boil and simmer for 15 minutes. Add the potatoes and cook for 10 minutes. Add the cauliflower and cashews. Cover and simmer until the cauliflower and potatoes are tender.

Meanwhile, in a skillet, sauté the 2 remaining onions in oil until golden brown. Add the cardamom and season with salt and pepper. Remove with a slotted spatula and drain on kitchen paper.

Stir the garam masala and crème fraiche into the cauliflower mixture. Transfer to a serving dish and top with the sautéed onions and coriander leaves.

FRESH FIG TART

Making this tart is a great way to use up any soft or less-than-perfect figs. The delicious combination of pastry, fruit and cream is best served warm.

Serves 6 to 8

150g (1¼ cups) plain (all-purpose) flour, sifted, plus more for work surface

Pinch salt

70g (5 tablespoons) unsalted butter

4 large eggs

30g (2 tablespoons plus 1 teaspoon) caster sugar

275g (1 cup) crème fraiche

1 tablespoon sweet wine

40g (⅓ cup) pine nuts, toasted

8 fresh figs, quartered

In a bowl, combine the sifted flour and salt, then rub in the butter until the mixture resembles coarse crumbs. Whisk 1 egg with 1 tablespoon cold water. Add to the flour mixture a little at a time, stirring it in with a fork, just until the dough forms a ball.

Roll the dough into a disk on a lightly floured work surface and use it to line a 22-cm (8½-inch) tart tin with a removeable bottom. Refrigerate for 30 minutes. Preheat the oven to 180°C (350°F).

Prick the bottom of the crust with a fork, line with parchment or foil, fill with baking beans or pie weights and bake for 20 minutes. Remove from the oven and remove the parchment and baking beans.

In a small bowl whisk the sugar, crème fraiche, wine and remaining 3 eggs. Scatter the pine nuts over the base. Arrange the figs on the pine nuts, then pour the egg mixture over the figs to fill the shell.

Bake until mixture sets and turns golden. Cool on a rack until just warm before removing from the tin.

COURGETTE WALNUT CAKE

In late summer, there is inevitably a courgette glut and this recipe offers a way of using some of the excess vegetables. For those with a sweet tooth, chocolate chunks could be incorporated in place of the nuts or as an addition.

Serves 6 to 8

60ml (¼ cup) sunflower oil, plus more for tin

450g (3¾ cups) plain (all-purpose) flour

2 teaspoons bicarbonate of soda

1 teaspoon sea salt

1 teaspoon baking powder

2 teaspoons ground cinnamon

10 walnut halves, roughly chopped

100g (¾ cup) pecans, chopped

3 large eggs

450g (2¼ cups) soft brown sugar

1 teaspoon vanilla extract

2 tablespoons treacle

450g (1 pound) courgettes (zucchini), grated

Grated zest of 1 lemon

Preheat the oven to 180°C (350°F). Oil a loaf tin, line with parchment and set aside. In a large bowl sift together the flour, bicarbonate of soda, salt, baking powder and cinnamon. Add the walnuts and pecans and toss to combine.

In a separate bowl whisk the eggs with the sugar. Add the 60ml (¼ cup) oil, vanilla extract and treacle and beat to combine well. Fold in the grated courgettes (zucchini) and lemon zest.

Fold the egg mixture into the dry ingredients until well combined with no dry spots remaining. Pour into the prepared tin.

Bake until a tester emerges clean, 45 to 50 minutes. Cool completely on a rack before removing from the tin.

CARAMEL CUSTARDS WITH BAKED PEARS AND BAY

Serves 6

225g (1 cup plus 2 tablespoons) caster sugar

250ml (1 cup) milk

500ml (2 cups) cream

7 egg yolks

6 ripe firm pears

600ml (2½ cups) Marsala

200ml (¾ cup plus 2 tablespoons) honey

Finely grated zest of 1 lemon

1 cinnamon stick

1 vanilla pod

Sprig of bay leaves

Preheat the oven to 130°C (275°F). Place 6 ramekins in a deep baking tray.

Place the sugar in a heavy saucepan with 50ml (¼ cup) of water and cook over low heat, stirring gently, until the sugar dissolves. Bring to a boil and cook until golden brown to make a caramel, approximately 5 minutes.

Meanwhile, place the milk and cream in a separate saucepan and warm through but do not boil. Add the caramel to the milk mixture in a thin stream and stir well to combine.

Beat the egg yolks in a bowl until pale and then add to the hot caramel in a thin stream, whisking constantly. Strain into a jug or pitcher and distribute evenly among the 6 ramekins in the baking tray.

Add boiling water to come halfway up the sides of the ramekins. Bake until the custard has just set, about 50 minutes. Allow to cool completely.

Raise the oven temperature to 200°C (400°F). Arrange the whole pears on a roasting tray with the stems facing upward. Combine the Marsala, honey, lemon zest, cinnamon, vanilla and bay sprig and pour over the pears.

Cover with foil and bake for 20 minutes. Remove the foil and bake until tender, about 20 additional minutes.

Arrange the pears on individual plates. Strain their syrup and pour it over them. Serve caramel custards on the side.

Winter

Pinhead Porridge

Cauliflower and Sweetcorn Chowder

Spiced Squash Tagine

Roast Brussels Sprout, Leek and Star Anise

Potato and Celeriac Gratin

Beef and Stout Casserole

Duck and Celeriac Pie

Pear Tarte Tatin

Chocolate Biscuit Cake

Rhubarb and Strawberry Crumble

The Gardens in Winter

As the winter months arrive, it's essential to prepare the gardens for colder weather. It is a myth that this is a quiet time of year, as the tasks are as plentiful as they are at other times of the year. There are mulching and pruning to be done, bulbs to be planted, planting schedules to be made and the following year's seeds to be chosen. Each year we allow the skeletons of our herbaceous plants to stand for as long as the winter allows, and their hollow stems provide a habitat for a diverse range of insect life. They also create beautiful, frosted silhouettes in the winter months. In late winter we begin cutting back the herbaceous borders, removing old growth and making room for the impending growth of spring. Larger landscaping projects can also be tackled while there is less growth in the garden.

We are fortunate to have erected some polytunnels in a previously unused yard behind the castle. This means we can keep up crop production throughout the year and continue a steady food supply to the kitchen. If you are fortunate enough to have the space, a domestic greenhouse is a good way to begin a yearlong productive garden.

Our winter pruning regime is key to helping maintain the health and vigour of many of our trees and shrubs. Each winter the team aim to remove the four Ds when pruning. Firstly, they remove dead, diseased and damaged wood. Lastly, they look for disorderly branches—these are branches that are crossing over another. This helps thin the canopy and improves air circulation, which in turn reduces the likelihood of disease occurring in the next season. Pruning helps shape the form of the trees and shrubs we grow. A good example of this is the formative pruning carried out on our gooseberry bushes. Gooseberries naturally spread; however, space is limited in our fruit cage. The team therefore prune the gooseberries into upward-facing buds to create narrow and tall bushes that are more compact but still very productive.

Opposite: Snow blanketing the upper garden with Saint Carthage's Cathedral in the background; pages 160–61: The chimneypiece in the Banqueting Hall was exhibited in the Medieval Court of the Great Exhibition of 1851. *Céad míle fáilte*, meaning 'one hundred thousand welcomes' in Gaelic, has been carved into the stone below the Cavendish family stag heads and the Devonshire family serpent; pages 174–75: The Sitting Room.

PINHEAD PORRIDGE

We source our pinhead oats from Flahavan's mill, which is also in County Waterford. The mill traces its roots back to 1795 and has perfected the art of manufacturing porridge oats. The mill exports around the world. The porridge is also delicious with dairy-free milks. It is best when the oats are left to soak overnight.

Serves 6

500ml (2 cups) milk

200g (1¼ cups) steel-cut oatmeal or

200g (2 cups) rolled oats

Brown sugar, honey, ground cinnamon, ground nutmeg and/or berries for topping

In a saucepan, combine the milk with 500ml (2 cups) water. Add the oats, cover and soak overnight in the refrigerator.

In the morning, put the pan of oats over low heat and cook, stirring frequently. When the porridge starts to blow occasional puffs of bubbles, it is ready.

Add a pinch of brown sugar and honey and a pinch of cinnamon or nutmeg. We also love to serve the porridge with berries on top.

CAULIFLOWER AND SWEETCORN CHOWDER

This warming chowder makes an excellent and filling lunch or a hearty starter. Serve with slices of Buttermilk Rosemary Focaccia (page 113) or Irish Soda Bread (page 69). Of course, you can adjust the amount of chilli depending on your taste.

Serves 8 as a main

Salt to taste

6 ears corn, shucked

Extra virgin olive oil for sautéing

2 onions, sliced

1 leek, trimmed and sliced

3 ribs celery, chopped

4 cloves garlic, peeled and crushed

1 green chilli, seeded and sliced

1 large head cauliflower, broken into florets

One 400-ml (14-ounce) tin coconut milk

1 litre (4 cups) vegetable stock

Juice of ½ lemon

6 spring onions, sliced

Chopped unsalted peanuts for garnish

Leaves of ½ bunch basil

Leaves of 1 bunch coriander

1 red chilli, seeded and sliced

Bring a large pot of water to a boil, salt, and cook the corn until tender, 30 to 40 minutes. Drain and cool, then shave the kernels off the cobs.

Heat a little olive oil in a large saucepan over medium heat and sauté the onions, leek and celery until soft. Season with salt. Add the garlic and chilli and cook for 2 additional minutes.

Add the cauliflower and coconut milk. Reserve about 2 tablespoons corn kernels and add the rest to the pot. Add the stock and bring to a boil, then simmer until the cauliflower is tender, about 15 minutes. Purée with an immersion blender, taste and adjust seasoning and add the lemon juice.

In a small skillet, heat a small amount of olive oil and char the reserved corn kernels. Add the spring onions and peanuts.

Divide the soup among individual serving bowls. Garnish with basil, coriander, sliced chilli and the corn mixture.

SPICED SQUASH TAGINE

2 red onions, thinly sliced

60ml (¼ cup) sunflower oil

800g (1¾ pounds) squash, diced

Seeds of 6 cardamom pods, ground

1 teaspoon ground coriander

½ teaspoon ground nutmeg

½ teaspoon ground ginger

½ teaspoon ground turmeric

Pinch saffron

2 cinnamon sticks

2 bay leaves

1 tablespoon runny honey

1 red chilli, seeded and chopped

Sea salt and freshly ground black pepper to taste

4 tablespoons (¼ cup) chopped parsley

1 litre (4 cups) vegetable stock, warm

Peel of ½ preserved lemon, diced

150g (⅓ cups) dried apricots, sliced

Leaves of 1 bunch coriander

20g (2 tablespoons) pine nuts, roasted

We serve this easy-to-make tagine with couscous, bulghur or quinoa. It makes an excellent pairing with Spiced Cauliflower and Potatoes (page 140) or can be served as a side dish with grilled and barbequed meats or fish.

Serves 8 as a main

In a casserole dish or Dutch oven, sauté the onions in sunflower oil until tender, about 10 minutes. Add the squash and cook for 5 minutes. Add the spices, bay leaves, honey and chilli. Season to taste. Add the parsley and cook, stirring, for 5 minutes. Add the stock and simmer for 10 minutes.

Add the preserved lemon peel and apricots and simmer until the squash is tender.

Remove and discard bay leaves and cinnamon sticks. Stir in the coriander and top with the pine nuts and serve in the casserole dish.

ROAST BRUSSELS SPROUT, LEEK AND STAR ANISE

Another vegetable that is plentiful throughout the winter is the Brussels sprout. Serve this dish alongside any winter dish or roasted meat; it is especially good with Potato and Celeriac Gratin (page 163).

Serves 6 as a side dish

Sea salt to taste

500g (1 pound) Brussels sprouts, trimmed and halved

200g (7 ounces) tender broccoli

30g (2 tablespoons) unsalted butter

4 small leeks, trimmed into 4-cm (1½-inch) lengths

4 red onions, quartered

30g (2 tablespoons plus 1 teaspoon) brown sugar

2 cinnamon sticks

2 star anise

Juice of 1 lemon

2 sweet apples, cored and sliced

Maple syrup to taste

50g (½ cup) toasted pecans, slivered

Coriander leaves for garnish

Preheat the oven to 200°C (400°F).

Bring a large saucepan of salted water to a boil and blanch the sprouts for 2 minutes. Drain, refresh in cold water, drain again and pat dry. Place in a roasting tray.

In a saucepan, melt the butter over medium heat. Add the leeks and onions, season with salt, and sauté gently for 5 minutes. Add the sugar, cinnamon and star anise and cook, stirring, until sugar is dissolved. Add the lemon juice and apples.

Pour the mixture over the sprouts and drizzle with maple syrup.

Roast until the sprouts are golden but still a little crunchy, about 15 minutes. Remove and discard cinnamon and star anise.

Scatter on the pecans and coriander leaves and serve.

POTATO AND CELERIAC GRATIN

This recipe elevates the trusty potato into an indulgence, making it a wonderful dish for spoiling guests when entertaining in winter.

Serves 8 as a side dish

75g (5 tablespoons) unsalted butter

1.5kg (3⅓ pounds) potatoes, peeled and thinly sliced

600g (1⅓ pounds) celeriac, peeled and thinly sliced

600ml (2½ cups) cream

900ml (3¾ cups) whole milk

3 cloves garlic, peeled and crushed

3 tablespoons prepared horseradish

Sea salt and freshly ground white pepper to taste

Preheat the oven to 200°C (400°F). Coat a large roasting tray with some of the butter.

Arrange a layer of sliced potatoes in the bottom of the tray. Make a layer of celeriac on top. Continue alternating layers, finishing with a layer of potatoes.

Mix the cream, milk, garlic and horseradish together and season the mixture with salt and pepper. Pour over the potatoes and celeriac.

Dot with the remaining butter and bake until the vegetables are tender and golden on top, about 1 hour. Allow to settle before serving.

BEEF AND STOUT CASSEROLE

500g (1 pound) shallots, peeled
and sliced

2 leeks, sliced

2 tablespoons extra virgin olive oil

6 cloves garlic, minced

200g (7 ounces) streaky bacon, diced

2kg (4½ pounds) stewing beef, cut
into cubes

50g (¼ cup plus 2 tablespoons) plain
(all-purpose) flour

2 tablespoons tomato purée

Leaves of 1 sprig thyme, chopped

1 bay leaf

Leaves of 1 small bunch parsley,
chopped

400ml (1⅔ cups) Murphy's or other
Irish stout

1 litre (4 cups) beef or vegetable stock
or a combination of the two

Sea salt and freshly ground black
pepper to taste

1 teaspoon Worcestershire sauce

4 carrots, peeled and roughly
chopped

75g (¼ cup plus 2 tablespoons)
pearl barley

6 large potatoes, roughly chopped

200g (7 ounces) baby button
mushrooms

Unsalted butter for sautéing

This recipe ties in two classic Irish products: beef and stout. We are lucky to have a high-quality local butcher in the village, and premium beef really makes all the difference to this slow-cooked casserole. Our stout of choice is Murphy's, which is brewed down the road in Cork. (Of course, the stout can be omitted if it's not appropriate for your guests.) Serve this with hefty chunks of bread or plain floury potatoes that you have boiled separately until tender.

Serves 8

In a casserole dish, sauté the shallots and leeks in olive oil for 5 minutes. Add the garlic and remove from the heat.

In a skillet, render the fat from the bacon. Remove the bacon with a slotted spoon and add to the shallots. Working in batches to avoid crowding, brown pieces of the beef in the bacon fat, then add them to the shallots as they are cooked. Add the flour to the mixture, stir to combine and cook over medium heat for 5 minutes.

Stir in the tomato purée, thyme and bay leaf. Reserve 1 to 2 tablespoons parsley for garnish and add the rest to the casserole dish. Stir in the stout and stock and season with salt, pepper and Worcestershire sauce. Give it all a good stir, then add the carrots and barley. Simmer for 1 hour.

Add the potatoes and simmer for 50 additional minutes. Meanwhile, sauté the mushrooms in butter until soft, then stir into the casserole and simmer for 10 additional minutes.

To serve, remove and discard bay leaf, then divide among individual bowls and garnish with reserved parsley.

DUCK AND CELERIAC PIE

½ bottle red wine

1 teaspoon chopped fresh rosemary leaves

1 teaspoon chopped fresh thyme leaves

1 tablespoon chopped parsley

8 large duck legs

2 onions, finely chopped

4 cloves garlic, crushed

2 tablespoons Worcestershire sauce

400g (1 pound) tomatoes, chopped

3 carrots, peeled and chopped

3 parsnips, peeled and chopped

1 tablespoon red currant jelly

Vegetable stock, as needed

1 celeriac, peeled and chopped

6 large potatoes, peeled and chopped

Sea salt to taste

100g (7 tablespoons) unsalted butter

2 tablespoons heavy cream

150ml (½ cup plus 2 tablespoons) whole milk

A pie is a classic winter dish in Ireland, and we choose to top this one with potatoes rather than pastry to pack in as many garden ingredients as possible. The duck is best when marinated overnight, so you will need to start this dish the day before you intend to serve it.

Serves 8 as a main

In a large bowl combine the red wine and herbs. Add the duck legs, cover and refrigerate for at least 8 hours.

Preheat the oven to 170°C (325°F). Remove the duck from the marinade, reserving the liquid. Pat the duck dry. Place a heavy skillet over high heat and sear the duck skin-side down to render the fat, working in batches if necessary. With tongs, lift the duck legs from the skillet and let any excess fat drain away. (Reserve the duck fat.) Transfer the duck to a large casserole dish, cover with foil and roast for 30 minutes.

Meanwhile, in a skillet sauté the onions and garlic in a little of the duck fat. Add the onion mixture to the casserole dish with the reserved marinade, Worcestershire sauce, tomatoes, carrots, parsnips and jelly. Cover and roast until the duck is very tender, about 1 hour. If the casserole begins to look dry before the duck is cooked, add vegetable stock in small amounts.

Allow the duck to cool in the sauce, then refrigerate for 1 hour. Meanwhile, cook the celeriac and potatoes in salted boiling water until tender. Drain and mash while still warm. Whisk in the butter, cream and milk and taste and adjust seasoning.

Preheat the oven to 200°C (400°F).

Discard any excess fat that solidified on top of the duck. Pick the meat from the legs. Discard the bones and combine the meat and the remaining contents of the casserole in a pie dish. Top with the potato mixture and bake until golden and bubbling, about 20 minutes.

PEAR TARTE TATIN

Pears remain in season through the early winter months and are therefore a great ingredient for a winter pudding. There are several varieties of pears growing in the garden—some are ornamental, and some are for cooking. We find that the conference, Concorde and Doyenné du Comice varieties are best for this tarte tatin.

Makes one 23-cm (9-inch) tart, serves 6 to 8

165g (¾ cup plus 1 tablespoon) caster sugar

65g (4 tablespoons) unsalted butter

1 teaspoon minced fresh thyme leaves

6 pears, halved, peeled and cored

One 10-inch circle puff pastry

Place a 23-cm (9-inch) ovenproof skillet over low heat. Combine the sugar and 100ml (¼ cup plus 2 tablespoons) water in the skillet and stir until the sugar has dissolved. Turn the heat up and simmer until the syrup turns golden brown.

Stir in the butter and thyme and cook to make a caramel.

Arrange the pears cut sides up around the pan to cover the caramel completely.

Place the puff pastry on top of the pears. Tuck the edges in around the perimeter of the skillet to surround the pears. Cut a slit in the puff pastry with a sharp knife.

Bake until the pastry is golden brown, about 40 minutes.

Allow to settle for a few minutes, then overturn a serving platter on top of the skillet. Flip both skillet and platter and lift off the skillet. (If any pears stick to the skillet, simply remove them and place them back on top of the tart.) Serve warm.

CHOCOLATE BISCUIT CAKE

A real treat, this rich chocolate biscuit cake can be kept in the fridge for a few days. Popular with adults and children alike, it is a teatime favourite.

Serves 6

120g (1 stick) butter, plus more for pan

300g (11 ounces) rich tea or digestive biscuits

80g (¼ cup plus 2 tablespoons) caster sugar

1 tablespoon plus 1 teaspoon cocoa powder

3 large eggs, beaten

150g (5 ounces) dark chocolate, chopped

100g (4 ounces) milk chocolate, chopped

Line a large loaf tin (approximately 30cm/12 inches long) with parchment paper and butter the base and edges.

Crush the biscuits as roughly or finely as you like and set aside.

In a saucepan combine the 120g (1 stick) butter and the sugar and cook over low heat until the butter has melted and the sugar has dissolved. Add the cocoa powder, stir and then remove from the heat and allow to cool.

Fold in the beaten eggs and the crushed biscuits. Spoon the mixture into the prepared tin and press down firmly.

Melt the two types of chocolate together in the top of a double boiler, stirring constantly. Pour the melted chocolate over the biscuit mix and spread evenly. Refrigerate for at least 2 hours before unmoulding and serving.

RHUBARB AND STRAWBERRY CRUMBLE

A winter staple—simple, delicious and easy to adapt. Use in-season fruits. We tend to have an abundance of berries during the summer harvest, some of which we freeze, and these can be added to a crumble later in the year.

Serves 6 to 8

300g rhubarb, cut into 5-cm chunks

250g strawberries, halved

Zest and juice of 1 orange

75g caster sugar

75g plain (all-purpose) flour

50g golden caster sugar

25g almonds, chopped

50g butter

Flaked almonds or pine nuts

Roast the rhubarb with the orange juice, zest and caster sugar uncovered at 180°C (356°F) for approximately 15 minutes until tender.

Add strawberries and cook for a further 5 minutes.

Place the roasted rhubarb and strawberries into a serving dish.

To make the Crumble Topping:

Mix the flour and sugar together and add the butter. Rub together to make coarse crumbs and add the almonds.

Spoon the crumble topping over the fruit and scatter over the flaked almonds and bake for 25 minutes until golden.

Serve with cream, ice cream or custard.

Chutneys & Jams

Beetroot Relish

Spicy Squash Chutney

Onion Marmalade

Irish Whiskey Marmalade

Sweet Chilli Jam

Mixed Tomato Chutney

Rhubarb and Orange Jam

Aronia and Strawberry Jam

Gooseberry and Elderflower Jam

BEETROOT RELISH

Serve this relish with a cheeseboard or with cold meats and pâtés. It is a good way to use up any beetroots that were not cooked early in the season. On page 126, we note how to store root vegetables through the colder months.

Makes four 220-ml (8-ounce) jars

1.5kg (3⅓ pounds) beetroot

1 teaspoon caster sugar

450g (1 pound) shallots, chopped

600ml (2½ cups) cider vinegar

1 tablespoon pickling spice, wrapped in a muslin bag

1 red chilli, finely chopped

2 teaspoons coriander seeds, crushed

450g (2¼ cups) granulated sugar

Place the beetroot in a large saucepan with the 1 teaspoon caster sugar. Add water to cover, bring to a boil and simmer until the beets are tender enough to pierce with a paring knife. Drain and allow to cool. Peel the cooled beets and cut into small cubes.

Place the shallots and vinegar in a preserving pan and cook over low heat for 10 minutes. Add the beetroot, pickling spice, chilli and coriander. Stir in the granulated sugar and cook gently until the sugar has dissolved. Bring to a boil and cook briskly for 5 minutes, then reduce the heat and simmer until the mixture thickens, approximately 40 additional minutes.

Remove the spice bag and ladle the mixture into sterilised jars. Seal hermetically with lids. Allow to mature for 1 month before using.

SPICY SQUASH CHUTNEY

This chutney is a wonderful complement to curries, as well as being a great addition to cheese and biscuits.

Makes six to eight 220-ml (8-ounce) jars

1 onion, peeled and diced

½ red chilli, minced

Seeds of 7 cardamom pods

1 teaspoon cumin seeds

2 cloves garlic, crushed

1½ teaspoons black mustard seeds

Sunflower oil for sautéing

50g (¼ cup) chopped ginger

500g (1 pound) butternut squash, peeled and diced

2 Bramley apples, cored, peeled and chopped

1 cinnamon stick

½ teaspoon ground turmeric

250g (1¼ cups) light brown sugar

150ml (⅔ cup) cider vinegar

1 teaspoon salt

Sauté the onion, chilli, cardamom, cumin seeds, garlic and mustard seeds in a large saucepan in sunflower oil until the spices are aromatic and the onions soften. Add the ginger, squash, apples and cinnamon stick and cook until the apples soften slightly, about 15 minutes. Add the turmeric and brown sugar, stir to coat the vegetables and simmer until the sugar has melted, about 5 minutes.

Pour in the vinegar and add the salt. Simmer until the apples have cooked down and the squash is tender but still holds its shape, about 30 minutes.

Spoon the chutney into hot sterilised jars and hermetically seal with lids.

ONION MARMALADE

In this recipe we have used white onions, but red onions are a delicious alternative.

Makes six to eight 220-ml (8-ounce) jars

750g (1⅔ pounds) white onions, thinly sliced

1 tablespoon fine sea salt

600g (3 cups) sugar

300ml (1¼ cups) red wine vinegar

½ teaspoon finely chopped fresh thyme leaves

Place the onions in a bowl with the salt. Cover and allow to rest at room temperature for 1 hour.

Rinse the onions in a colander and drain thoroughly.

Put the sugar and vinegar in a large pan and simmer over low heat until the sugar has dissolved. Add the onions and the thyme, bring to a boil and then simmer gently until the syrup is thick and the onions are translucent, about 2 hours.

Spoon straight into sterilised jars and hermetically seal with lids.

IRISH WHISKEY MARMALADE

In Ireland, we make this in January to catch the Seville orange season. Use your whiskey of choice. This marmalade is delicious on a slice of Irish Soda Bread (page 69).

Makes six to eight 220-ml (8-ounce) jars

600g (1⅓ pounds) Seville oranges

1 lemon

400g (2 cups) granulated sugar

200ml (¾ cup plus 2 tablespoons) Irish whiskey

Cut the oranges and lemon in half and juice them. Scoop out the pulp and wrap it in muslin. Tie closed with kitchen twine.

Put the peels, juice and muslin bag in a large pot with 2 litres (8 cups) water and bring to a boil. Simmer until the liquid is reduced by one third and the fruit is soft, 1 to 1½ hours.

Remove the fruit peels, allow to cool and slice as fine or thick as you would like your marmalade chunks to be. Return the peels to the pan and remove the muslin bag with the pulp.

Meanwhile, spread the sugar on a baking tray and warm in an oven on low heat.

Bring the mixture back to a boil and add the sugar. Stir until the sugar dissolves. Add the whiskey and bring to a rolling boil until the mixture reaches the setting point of 104°C (219°F).

Pour straight into sterilised warm jars and hermetically seal with lids.

SWEET CHILLI JAM

This jam is a great addition to the table to add a subtle spicy kick. The heat level can vary based on the type and amount of chilli used, so adjust as you prefer. A jar of this jam makes a wonderful house present for friends or neighbours.

Makes six to eight 220-ml (8-ounce) jars

---

6 large red chillies

75g (⅓ cup) grated ginger

5 cloves garlic

600g (1⅓ pounds) ripe tomatoes

350g (1¾ cups) caster sugar

150ml (½ cup plus 2 tablespoons) red wine vinegar

50ml (3 tablespoons plus 1 teaspoon) nam pla

Place the chillies, ginger, garlic and tomatoes in a food processor fitted with the metal blade and pulse until puréed.

Dissolve the sugar in the vinegar in a large saucepan and bring to a boil. Add the chilli purée and return to a boil. Add the nam pla. Simmer until the mixture thickens and reaches a jamlike consistency, about 30 minutes.

Pour into sterilised jars, cover and allow to cool, then seal hermetically.

MIXED TOMATO CHUTNEY

We have several varieties of tomato growing at Lismore. This is in large part thanks to Mervyn Hobbs—a member of the gardening team for twelve years—who began cross-breeding tomatoes a few years ago.

Most recently Mervyn decided to cross the Cherokee purple, which is a tasty beefsteak tomato, with the blue fire tomato, which Mervyn is particularly fond of for its vivid colours. The result was a delicious new beefsteak tomato which has taken on the colour of the blue fire, and the size of the Cherokee purple. While it has been a success, this new variety occasionally splits once ripe. However, this makes it ideal for chutney making, since there is no reason for tomatoes going into chutney to look perfect.

Makes six to eight 220-ml (8-ounce) jars

1kg (2¼ pounds) mixed tomatoes, chopped

300g (11 ounces) cooking apples, about 2 medium, peeled, cored and chopped

3 white onions, peeled and chopped

2 cloves garlic, minced

1½ teaspoons sea salt

2 tablespoons pickling spice

600ml (2½ cups) apple cider vinegar

300g (1½ cups) granulated sugar

Combine all the ingredients in a large pot and bring to a simmer. Cook, stirring frequently, until thick and pulpy, about $1\frac{1}{2}$ hours.

Pour into sterilised jars and hermetically seal.

RHUBARB AND ORANGE JAM

We make this using an Irish rhubarb variety grown on the castle grounds for generations. The addition of orange cuts through the acidity of the rhubarb.

Makes six to eight 220-ml (8-ounce) jars

1kg (2¼ pounds) rhubarb, cut into 1-cm (½-inch) pieces

1kg (5 cups) granulated sugar

Finely grated zest and juice of 1 orange

1 cinnamon stick

On a baking tray combine the rhubarb, sugar, zest, juice and cinnamon stick. Leave at room temperature for at least 8 hours.

Transfer the ingredients to a saucepan and stir while bringing to a gentle simmer.

Bring to a rolling boil and boil until the mixture reaches the setting point of 104°C (219°F) on a jam thermometer. Remove and discard cinnamon stick.

Pour into sterilised jars and hermetically seal.

ARONIA AND STRAWBERRY JAM

Aronia berries, also called chokeberries, have a distinctively sharp, sour taste which is why they work so well with strawberries in this jam recipe. If you can't find aronia berries near you, black currants or blueberries work as a substitute.

Makes six to eight 220-ml (8-ounce) jars

360g (13 ounces) aronia berries

500g (1 pound) strawberries, hulled and halved

1kg (5 cups) granulated sugar

Combine the aronia berries and 200ml ($\frac{3}{4}$ cup plus 2 tablespoons) water in a large pan and bring to a boil. Cook until the berries start to break down. Add the strawberries. Meanwhile, spread the sugar on a baking tray and warm in a low oven. When the strawberries start to break down, add the sugar.

Cook until the mixture reaches the setting point of 104°C (219°F) on a jam thermometer.

Pour straight into sterilised jars and hermetically seal.

GOOSEBERRY AND ELDERFLOWER JAM

Sharp gooseberries and fragrant elderflowers are in season at the same time in early summer and complement each other in this marriage of flavours.

Makes six to eight 220-ml (8-ounce) jars

1.2kg (2⅔ pounds) gooseberries, topped and tailed

1.4kg (7 cups) sugar

8 elderflower heads or 100ml (¼ cup plus 2 tablespoons) Elderflower Cordial (page 212)

Combine the gooseberries with 400ml (1⅔ cups) water in a large pan and boil until the gooseberries start to break apart.

Meanwhile, spread the sugar on a baking tray and warm in a low oven.

When the gooseberries are broken down, add the sugar and stir until it dissolves, then add the elderflower heads. Return to a boil and cook, stirring frequently, until the mixture turns pink and reaches the setting point of 104°C (219°F) on a jam thermometer.

Use tongs to remove the elderflower heads and discard them.

Pour the jam straight into sterilised warm jars and hermetically seal with lids.

Fermenting

An Introduction to Fermentation
By Kelly Mason

Fermentation is a process by which sugars, or carbohydrates, are converted into a combination of acids, gases and alcohol by way of bacteria or yeast. The process of fermentation is a form of digestion performed under anaerobic conditions. We know of the many health benefits to the gut from foods that have undertaken the fermentation process, so we have included a few recipes for you to experiment with the process.

Kombucha

The fermentation process for tonic beverages such as kombucha or kefir requires what is called a starter culture or a SCOBY, which stands for 'symbiotic colony of bacteria and yeast'.

These bubbly, very slightly alcoholic tonics produce numerous organic acids, nutrients and minerals during their digestive process. The result is a fizzy probiotic drink that contains millions of live cultures. These support gut health and aid in creating healthy digestive and immune systems.

A slightly tangy probiotic drink, kombucha is a fermented, sweetened tea. It can be drunk as a shot after the first ferment or taken to a second ferment to create a fizzy fruit-flavoured beverage. Most ingredients needed to create kombucha can be found in your local supermarket.

KOMBUCHA

Makes 1 jar

60g (¼ cup plus 1 heaping tablespoon) organic caster sugar

3 organic Earl Grey tea bags

2 organic breakfast tea bags

1 SCOBY, plus 100ml (¼ cup plus 2 tablespoons) kombucha liquid (if you purchase SCOBY, this usually comes with it)

For the first ferment, combine the sugar and 1 litre (4 cups) of boiling water in a pan and heat, stirring, until the sugar is dissolved. Add the tea bags and infuse for 5 minutes.

Remove the tea bags and allow the tea to cool completely.

Tip the cooled tea into a sterilised 2-litre (8-cup) kilner jar with the SCOBY and kombucha liquid, then cover the top with a muslin cloth and fix in place with an elastic band.

Set aside in a cool, dark place until fermented, 1 to 2 weeks.

Note: Each time you make a new first ferment batch of kombucha, remove the SCOBY and 100ml (¼ cup plus 2 tablespoons) of the liquid to use for the next batch.

You can refrigerate the fermented drink and consume it within a couple of days, or you can continue to ferment a second time, flavouring it with fruit.

Second Ferment

RASPBERRY KOMBUCHA

150g (5 ounces) frozen raspberries

2 tablespoons runny honey

750ml (3 cups) first ferment kombucha

In a small pan, combine the raspberries and honey and heat over low heat until soft. Strain through a fine sieve and leave to cool completely.

Mix the raspberry purée with the first ferment kombucha. Pour into a sterilised fliptop kilner bottle and seal.

Set aside in a cool, dark place until sweet, sour and lightly carbonated, 2 days to 1 week. Refrigerate for up to 1 week.

STRAWBERRY AND LIME KOMBUCHA

200g (7 ounces) strawberries

Zest and juice of 2 unwaxed limes

1 tablespoon runny honey

750ml (3 cups) first ferment kombucha

In a food processor fitted with the metal blade, combine the strawberries, lime zest and juice and honey, and purée.

Strain through a fine sieve into a large jug, then mix in the first ferment kombucha. Pour into a sterilised fliptop kilner bottle and seal.

Set aside in a cool, dark place until sweet, sour and lightly carbonated, 2 days to 1 week. Refrigerate for up to 1 week.

KIMCHI

Kimchi is a staple in Korean cuisine and boasts numerous probiotics—healthy microorganisms that help regulate the immune system and fight inflammation. Add a spoonful to eggs in the morning or to enliven a salad, or simply enjoy it on toast.

Makes 1 kilner jar

1 head Napa cabbage, quartered

About 1 tablespoon sea salt

½ red bell pepper, seeded

2 tablespoons tamari

2 tablespoons coconut sugar

4 tablespoons (¼ cup) chopped ginger

¼ cup peeled garlic cloves

2 shallots

1 red chilli

60ml (¼ cup) pineapple juice

¼ cup thinly sliced radish (optional)

¼ cup julienned spring onions (optional)

¼ cup julienned carrots (optional)

1 teaspoon dried chilli flakes (optional)

The entire cooking area, all utensils and your hands must be sanitised throughout the process.

Place the cabbage wedges in a large mixing bowl and pack generous amounts of sea salt between the leaves, massaging it into them.

Place a plate or pot lid on top, weight it down and allow the cabbage to sit for at least 30 minutes. This softens and breaks down the cabbage and draws out moisture so that it can be brined effectively.

In a food processor fitted with the metal blade, combine the bell pepper, tamari, coconut sugar, ginger, garlic, shallots and red chilli. Combine with the pineapple juice and 60ml (¼ cup) warm water.

Toss this liquid with the cabbage and any of the optional ingredients. Transfer to a sterilised kilner jar and press until all the ingredients are submerged in the liquid. Seal and allow to ferment in a cool, dry place for at least 36 hours or ferment in the refrigerator for up to 1 week. (The latter produces more flavourful kimchi.) Once a day while the kimchi is fermenting, open the jar and press down with a clean utensil to expel air bubbles and ensure the vegetables are submerged in liquid.

RED CABBAGE
KIMCHI

Makes 1 kilner jar

---

1 head red cabbage, quartered

About 3 tablespoons sea salt

5 cloves garlic, minced

4 tablespoons (¼ cup) minced ginger

4 tablespoons (¼ cup) gochugaru

2 tablespoons tamari

2 tablespoons coconut sugar

1 red chilli

60ml (¼ cup) pineapple juice

The entire cooking area, all utensils and your hands must be sanitised throughout the process.

Place the cabbage wedges in a large mixing bowl and pack generous amounts of sea salt between the leaves, massaging it into them.

Place a plate or pot lid on top, weight it down and allow the cabbage to sit for at least 30 minutes. This softens and breaks down the cabbage and draws out moisture so that it can be brined effectively.

In a food processor fitted with the metal blade, pulse the garlic, ginger, gochugaru, tamari, coconut sugar and chilli to combine. Combine with the pineapple juice and 60ml (¼ cup) warm water.

Toss this liquid with the cabbage quarters. Transfer to a sterilised kilner jar and press until all the ingredients are submerged in the liquid. Seal and allow to ferment in a cool, dry place for at least 36 hours or ferment in the refrigerator for up to 1 week. (The latter produces more flavourful kimchi.) Once a day while the kimchi is fermenting, open the jar and press down with a clean utensil to expel air bubbles and ensure the vegetables are submerged in liquid.

Drinks & Cocktails

Our Homegrown Apple Juice

Elderflower Cordial

The Astaire

Lismore's Cosmopolitan

Bloody Mary with Homemade Tomato Juice

Irish Whiskey Sour

Iced Baileys

OUR HOMEGROWN
APPLE JUICE

The apples are picked in the autumn and sent to a local apple farm for juicing. The farm is called The Apple Farm and is owned by Con Traas, whose family have been growing apples in the area since 1968. The minimum quantity of apples that are required for juicing is 600 kilograms (more than 1,300 pounds). The total amount we harvest varies but always exceeds this minimum.

When there is a full team of gardeners able to focus on apple picking for a few days each year, we average around 1,000 bottles of apple juice. The bottles are returned within a month ready to be used in the castle and sold in the café and shop.

There are approximately twenty-five different varieties of apples in the orchard. Almost all the apples are used for juice, with the exception of some apples that Teena takes for baking and chutneys. Occasionally there can be too many cooking apples going into the juice; this results in a slightly tart taste which some people prefer. This year we have planted more dessert apples to counter this, but it is a balance that needs to be managed each year. In the meantime, the apple juice has a unique flavour which is still very pleasing.

ELDERFLOWER CORDIAL

This recipe makes a generous amount of cordial. If you bottle the early-blooming elderflowers, which have the best flavour, the cordial can last you through the rest of the summer. Once made, it will keep for 6 months in the fridge and can also be frozen. Serve with mineral or sparkling water, a tonic or sparkling fizz as you prefer.

Makes 4 litres (1 gallon)

2kg (10 cups) granulated sugar

50g (3 tablespoons plus 1½ teaspoons) citric acid

Zest and juice of 2 lemons

20 elderflower heads

In a pan combine 2.5 litres (2⅔ quarts) water, the sugar and the citric acid. Cook, stirring, until dissolved. Add the lemon zest and juice and the flowers. Allow to cool.

Transfer to a container with a tight-fitting lid and refrigerate for 2 to 3 days, stirring daily.

Strain the liquid through a fine sieve. Pour into sterilised bottles and refrigerate.

THE ASTAIRE

We use our homegrown apple juice in our Champagne cocktail, but you can use any apple juice not made from concentrate. A chic cocktail which is very easy to make, it is best enjoyed on a warm evening.

Makes 1 cocktail

50ml (1½ ounces/1 shot) Champagne

30ml (1 ounce/1 short shot) apple juice

1 lemon twist

Combine the Champagne and apple juice in a cocktail shaker and very gently shake for a few seconds. Pour into a glass and garnish with the twist of lemon.

LISMORE'S COSMOPOLITAN

We offer a classic cosmopolitan though with a little flair in its presentation. Pick seasonal flowers—we often use rose blossoms in the summer and holly in the winter—and press them up against the inside of a saucepan. Hold them in place with a bowl slightly smaller than the pan. Pour boiling water into the gap between the bowl and pan to cover the flowers. Freeze overnight. The following day, when the cocktail mix has been prepared, remove the bowl to reveal a beautiful ice container with pressed flowers frozen inside it. The container should slide out of the pan and is ready to hold several servings of cosmopolitan.

Makes 1 cocktail

50ml (1½ ounces/1 shot) lemon vodka

25ml (¾ ounce/½ shot) triple sec

25ml (¾ ounce/½ shot) lime juice

50ml (1½ ounces/1 shot) cranberry juice

1 orange twist

Combine vodka, triple sec, lime juice and cranberry juice in a shaker. Shake to combine, then strain into an ice bowl. To serve, ladle into a glass and garnish with the orange twist.

BLOODY MARY WITH HOMEMADE TOMATO JUICE

We make our bloody mary with homemade tomato juice and have included the recipe here. You need a large number of tomatoes to make the juice—a great way to use up a surplus. Since the tomatoes will be blended, toss in any misfit, odd-shaped tomatoes and those that have split while growing. Ripe tomatoes are a must. This recipe will make enough juice for about three cocktails—it's not worth making it in quantities smaller than that.

Makes 1 cocktail

Tomato Juice

1.5kg (3⅓ pounds) very ripe tomatoes, cored and roughly chopped

125g (3 medium ribs) celery, chopped

35g (⅓ cup) white onion, chopped

2 tablespoons sugar

1 teaspoon salt

Pinch black pepper

-

Cocktail

50ml (1½ ounces/1 shot) vodka

200ml (¾ cup plus 2 tablespoons) tomato juice

10ml (2 teaspoons) Worcestershire sauce

Tabasco to taste

Pinch salt and freshly ground black pepper

1 rib celery

For the tomato juice, combine all of the ingredients in a large pot, bring to a simmer and simmer uncovered for 25 minutes. Strain and allow to cool completely.

For the cocktail, combine the vodka, tomato juice and Worcestershire sauce in a glass and stir. Add a dash of tabasco and season with salt and pepper. Garnish with the celery.

IRISH WHISKEY SOUR

Use your Irish whiskey of choice in this favourite mix. It combines the smooth, honeyed notes of whiskey with the tangy zip of lemon juice—freshly squeezed juice is essential. The result is a cocktail that's both bold and balanced. It can be enjoyed by the fire on a chilly evening or on a warm summer day to toast the Emerald Isle. You can replace the egg white with aquafaba (chickpea water) to make a vegan cocktail.

Makes 1 cocktail

50ml (1½ ounces/1 shot) whiskey

35ml (1¼ ounces) freshly squeezed lemon juice

1 egg white

3 dashes Angostura bitters

12.5ml (2½ teaspoons) 2:1 sugar syrup

Combine the whiskey, lemon juice and egg white in a cocktail shaker and shake without ice for 30 seconds. Fill the shaker halfway with ice and shake again.

Strain into a glass over one large ice cube. Add Angostura.

ICED BAILEYS

This sweet and indulgent cocktail is a perfect treat for coffee lovers. A famous Irish brand, Baileys is still produced on Irish soil. Leonard ingeniously pours melted chocolate down the sides of the glass before chilling it for an extra touch.

Makes 1 cocktail

Melted chocolate for glass

50ml (1½ ounces/1 shot) Baileys Irish cream

50ml (1½ ounces/1 shot) vodka

Chill a martini glass in the fridge. Pour the melted chocolate down the side of the glass and chill until set.

Fill a cocktail shaker halfway with ice and add the Baileys and vodka. Shake well to combine and strain into the prepared glass.

BED RM 1   BED RM 2   BED RM 3   EAST WING
                                  BED RM 4   BED RM 5   DINING RM

EAST WING
BATH RM   SMOKE RM   BED RM   FLAG TOWER
                              BATH RM   LR BEDROOM   BATH RM 1   BATH

COURT YARD
BED RM 1   BED RM 2   LIBRARY   HALL   ANTE RM   DRAWING RM   DINING

Flowers

Just as with food, we take a seasonal approach to flowers in the house at Lismore. When spring emerges, the first hellebores come up, and this signals the beginning of the new season. There are several different arrangements in the house; as you come into the entrance hall, we usually have a large vase on the table, and in that I really like to have a great abundance of just one thing. This might mean a few branches of a *Magnolia stellata* or *Camelia* 'Alba Plena' (which remains a particular favourite as I wore it in my hair on my wedding day). As the season goes on *Thalictrum*, giant fennel (*Ferula communis*) and physic purple (*Eryngium pandanifolium*) bought from Great Dixter Gardens all take their place in the large vase in the hall. For special occasions, a good trick I have adopted from the master florist Shane Connolly is to place a number of glass vases of different heights quite close to each other. This allows you to make a substantial arrangement without the use of floral foam.

In every bedroom beside the bed or on top of the chest of drawers there is an opportunity to have a smaller, more controlled arrangement. In spring this often means tulips, for which I have always had a strange passion. No doubt I would have traded my worldly belongings for a single bulb if I had been born in fifteenth-century Holland. My current favourites include the early-blooming ice stick, which seems to last well, with a pleasing pale petal and a flash of yellow in its interior, and the almost white concerto. I'm also fond of the blowsy, intense claret of palmyra and Uncle Tom or Ronaldo tulips. We have a selection of small ceramic vases for this purpose, many of them from Wemyss Ware and collected in recent years by my father-in-law.

In the centre of the dining room table, we have a multi-articulated ceramic planter by the Brazilian ceramicist Carina Ciscato in which I like to arrange what William refers to as 'hedgerow chic'. This consists of wafty perennials which usually don't make terribly good cut flowers because they don't last very long, but in my mind there is a place for something that is wonderful even just for a single day, and this vessel manages to hold them upright.

I have become more and more passionate about plants in the house, a sustainable alternative to cut flowers and relatively easy to look after; *Pelargonium* 'Lord Bute', dark prince and attar of roses geraniums

are easily bought in many garden centres, but for something more unusual try *Pelargonium triste*. I am reliably informed that it was the first *Pelargonium* to reach Europe from the cape of South Africa in the early seventeenth century. I am also a fan of the dark-leaved African geranium (*Pelargonium sidoides*).

In winter, as well as the usual Christmas fare of hollies and fir, we have a collection of orchids with names like *Dendrobium paxtonii* and *Stanhopea devoniensis* in well-worn terracotta pots that have found their way over to Ireland from Chatsworth. They are from the historic collection gathered by Paxton from all over the world in the mid-nineteenth century. A grouping on a table is a beautiful thing, and they are a reminder to me that through a tradition of care and nurturing they have managed to survive for a very long time—just like the castle.

- Laura Burlington

Floral Arrangements
through the Seasons

Like anything in gardening, there is an art to creating floral arrangements. Each different season poses its own challenges and unique opportunities for expressing the individual beauty of each season. When it comes to winter, less is often more. For example, a bunch of branches dressed in lichen can be just enough. Thankfully spring is always just around the corner and full of promise. The first green shoot always lifts the mood, bulbs begin to emerge from sodden winter soils and our garden landscapes begin to transform into picturesque flower pictures once again. Shrubs begin to bloom and fill the air with scent reminding you it's time to start sowing your summer annuals for the cutting garden.

The first spring arrangements should always celebrate the new growing season with heaving arrangements full of narcissus, hellebore, tulips and blossom branches taking centre stage in our vessels. The desired look should appear effortless and natural, nothing too stiff or forced. As our bulbs and bluebells begin to diminish, the season shifts into summer, plants in the garden begin to tower over our heads and long stems are celebrated with extra large arrangements filling the castle's interior with the abundance of summer. I love creating different moments in each room of the castle with the strategic use of certain plants, colour and texture no matter the season.

Summer seems to travel by at lightning pace for the working gardener, and the mellowness autumn brings is always welcomed. The days are still warm and the light is golden and hazy. This is one of my favourite seasons to get creative with the full fruition of the growing season, combining fruits, flowers and seeds in each vessel, attempting to create a similar feeling indoors. All of the seasons have something to offer, and each new cycle of growing season provides more opportunities for learning and making adjustments to plans for new plants, preventing arrangements from becoming stale and predictable. This not only makes me happy and content, but I'm always humbled to know that each new season allows me to have another go.

- Lee Behegan
  Gardener, Lismore Castle

Bibliography

Bence-Jones, Mark. 'Along the Valley of the Irish Rhine: The Blackwater – I', *Country Life*, 21 November 1963, 1328–30.

Chatsworth Collection and Archive, Bakewell, Derbyshire.

Colquhoun, Kate. *A Thing in Disguise: The Visionary Life of Joseph Paxton* (New York: HarperCollins, 2004).

Devonshire, Andrew. *Accidents of Fortune* (London: Michael Russell Publishing, 2004).

Girouard, Mark. 'Lismore Castle, Co Waterford – I', *Country Life*, 6 August 1964, 336–40.

Girouard, Mark. 'Lismore Castle, Co Waterford – II', *Country Life*, 13 August 1964, 389–93.

Hunter, Michael. *Boyle: Between God and Science* (New Haven and London: Yale University Press, 2009).

Jenkins, Elizabeth. *Lady Caroline Lamb* (London: Victor Gollancz, 1932).

Lambert, Elizabeth. 'Lismore's Next Chapter', *Architectural Digest*, January 2006, 144–53, 202.

Lees-Milne, James. *The Bachelor Duke: A Life of William Spencer Cavendish, 6th Duke of Devonshire, 1790–1858* (London: John Murray, 1991).

There has been a rich tradition of saving seeds in the garden in Lismore, and the team continue to save seeds from as wide a range of plants as possible — it is one of the most rewarding jobs we do. It is a key part of the sustainability credentials of the garden, as it not only cuts down on costs, but it also generates revenue and, more important, contributes to conservation initiatives at a national level in Ireland. In recent years, the garden team have started to grow out vegetable seed crops as part of the Irish Seed Savers Association Seed Guardian program, which aims to protect and preserve open pollinated, heritage and heirloom seeds. Plants grown from seeds saved in the garden often prove to be better adapted to the local climatic conditions within Lismore and as a result are often more resilient than shop-bought seeds.

At right: The Sundial Garden. Laura worked with Matthew Tull in 2009 to create a new feel in this part of the garden as a surprise for William's birthday. It was planted with the idea of reimagining what the sixth Duke would have seen when he arrived at the castle, semi-derelict but full of romance and overgrown with luscious plants. Out of shot it features curved oak benches by Henry Brudenell-Bruce.

Acknowledgements

Part of the motivation for making this book was to have the opportunity to acknowledge the hard work and commitment of everyone who works to make Lismore the place that it is. Denis Nevin has managed the castle and has looked after its guests for almost fifty years and is now joined by his sons, Patrick and Tony. Together with Michael Rafferty, Leonard Coleman and Jake Coleman they care for our visitors in the summer months, and the rest of the year turn their hands to essential maintenance in the house and beyond.

Food has always been an important part of the Lismore experience. It has been a great pleasure to make this book with Teena Mahon, the castle cook, who has created these recipes with diligence and enthusiasm. Her predecessor, Beth-Ann Smith of the Lismore Food Company, cooked for us when we first took over Lismore and taught me much of what I know about food for celebration and companionship. The fermentation section of the book was written by Kelly Mason, who has been generous in sharing her knowledge in this area.

After taking over the responsibility of this well-loved garden from my parents-in-law, we were lucky enough to employ Darren Topps as head gardener, and he remained with us for nine years. He was instrumental in the garden's recent development and laid the foundations that Colm O'Driscoll has so successfully taken forward. In this book you will see many of the garden team that includes Lee Behegan, Mervyn Hobbs, Declan Moher, Declan McPhillips and Sean Walsh, who have contributed to the horticultural tips. The office, headed up by Helen Courtney, alongside Ann Walsh and Breda Geoghegan, is at the core of the goings-on at Lismore and has run like clockwork under their watch since 2008. All of this activity has been overseen by Ben Heyes, who has been a valued member of the Devonshire Group team for over thirty years.

In a house such as Lismore, pests and dust remain a constant threat, and Norma Walsh, Tricia Feeney and Caroline Coleman keep these at bay. I must also thank Cat, who keeps the mouse population under control—the numbers are substantially less since he took up residence in the woodshed.

Paul McAree has run Lismore Castle Arts with dedication and imagination and has somehow found the time to design this book, which benefits from intimate knowledge of the place. He follows in the footsteps of Eamon Maxwell, who did much to establish the gallery's reputation.

I would like to say a special thank you to Eliza Wood, without whom this book would not have happened. She has run this project with her usual efficiency and light touch, and working with Anna Batchelor, the photographer, they have captured the essence of the place.

Lismore is shaped by the people who care for it, but also by those who move through it. William and I would like to thank all those visitors, guests, artists and writers who have helped us to maintain and sustain this wonderful building and fill it full of inspiration, education and conversation.

A final thank you to Charles Miers at Rizzoli for his support and belief, as ever.

First published in the United States of America in 2025
by Rizzoli International Publications, Inc.
49 West 27th Street
New York, NY 10001
www.rizzoliusa.com

For Rizzoli International Publications, Inc.
Publisher: Charles Miers
Production Manager: Alyn Evans

For Lismore Castle
Editor: Eliza Wood
Book designer: Paul McAree
Photography stylist: Tamineh Dhondy, pp. 68, 70, 75, 76,
78, 82, 87, 99, 101, 102, 106, 109, 112, 114, 119, 121, 129, 130,
134, 136, 139, 141, 144, 146, 149, 155, 157, 159, 164, 167, 168,
170, 173, 200, 203, 204, 207

Additional photography credits
pp. 33, 142–43, 150, 153: Photography © 2025 Paul McAree
pp. 246–47: Photography © 2025 Ros Kavanagh
pp. 28 (top and middle, left): Photography courtesy of
Country Life / Future Publishing Ltd.

Artwork credits
p. 33
Richard Wright
No title, 2011
Acrylic on wall, site-specific installation at Lismore
Castle. Dimensions variable. © Richard Wright,
courtesy Gagosian, London, and The Modern Institute /
Toby Webster Ltd, Glasgow.

pp. 246–47
Rashid Johnson
Untitled, 2018
Shea Butter Cast, unique
43.2 × 30.5 × 30.3 cm. Steel Base: 121.9 × 61 × 61 cm
Installation view at Lismore Castle Arts, 2018.
© Rashid Johnson. Courtesy the artist and Hauser &
Wirth

Additional captions
Front and Back Cover: The Upper Garden at
    Lismore Castle.
Endpapers: Bespoke wallpaper block-printed by
Cole & Son with the Cavendish family motto, *Cavendo
Tutus* (safety through caution), and elements from their
coat of arms.
pp. 4–5: Yew Tree Avenue, lower garden.
pp. 6–7: Lismore Castle viewed from the River
Blackwater.
pp. 8–9: Teena Mahon, the cook at Lismore Castle, in
the old kitchen.
pp. 10–11: Mervyn Hobbs in the vegetable beds.
p. 227: An out-of-use service board in the Butler's
Pantry.
pp. 250–51: Looking into the courtyard from the
sitting room.

ISBN: 978-0-8478-4417-3
Library of Congress Control Number:
9780847844173

Printed in China
2025 2026 2027 2028 / 10 9 8 7 6 5 4 3 2 1

Visit us online:
Instagram.com/RizzoliBooks
Facebook.com/RizzoliNewYork
X: @Rizzoli_Books
Youtube.com/user/RizzoliNY

MIX
Paper | Supporting
responsible forestry
FSC® C008047